Designed and Edited by William Mann
Copyright © 2021 mannwilliam.org
ISBN 9798501451537

KEATS

SHELLEY

BYRON

from

MAIN CURRENTS IN NINETEENTH CENTURY LITERATURE

BY

GEORGE BRANDES

IN SIX VOLUMES

IV

NATURALISM IN ENGLAND

EDITED BY
WILLIAM MANN

mannwilliam.org

CONTENTS

KEATS

ALL-EMBRACING SENSUOUSNESS

IN KEATS'S MAGNIFICENT FRAGMENT, *Hyperion,* there is a scene in which the whole overthrown race of Titanic gods hold counsel in a dark, underground cavern. Their chief, old Saturn, concludes his despondent speech with the words:

> Yet ye are here,
> O'erwhelm'd and spurred, and batter'd, ye are here!
> O Titans, shall I say, 'Arise!'—Ye groan:
> Shall I say 'Crouch!'—Ye groan. What can I then?
> O Heaven wide! O unseen parent dear!
> What can I? Tell me, all ye brethren Gods,
> How we can war, how engine our great wrath!"

Then Oceanus, the thoughtful, meditative sea god, rises, shakes his locks, no longer watery, and, in the murmuring voice which his tongue has caught from the break of the waves on the shore, bids the passion-stung deities take comfort from the thought that they have fallen by the course of Nature's law, and not by the force of thunder or of Jove:—

> Great Saturn, thou
> Hast sifted well the atom-universe;
> But for this reason, that thou art the King,
> And only blind from sheer supremacy,
> One avenue was shaded from thine eyes,
> Through which I wandered to eternal truth.
> And first, as thou wast not the first of powers,
> So art thou not the last; it cannot be:
> Thou art not the beginning nor the end.
> From Chaos and parental Darkness came
> Light, the first fruits of that intestine broil,
> That sullen ferment, which for wondrous ends
> Was ripening in itself. The ripe hour came,
> And with it light, and light engendering
> Upon its own producer, forthwith touch'd
> The whole enormous matter into life.
> Upon that very hour, our parentage,
> The Heavens and the Earth, were manifest:

> Then thou first-born, and we the giant race,
> Found ourselves ruling new and beauteous realms.
> Now comes the pain of truth, to whom 'tis pain;
> O folly! for to bear all naked truths,
> And to envisage circumstance, all calm,
> That is the top of sovereignty. Mark well!
> As Heaven and Earth are fairer, fairer far
> Than Chaos and blank Darkness, though once chiefs;
> And as we show beyond that Heaven and Earth
> In form and shape compact and beautiful,
> In will, in action free, companionship,
> And thousand other signs of purer life;
> So on our heels a fresh perfection treads,
> A power more strong in beauty, born of us
> And fated to excel us, as we pass
> In glory that old Darkness: nor are we
> Thereby more conquer'd, than by us the rule
> Of shapeless Chaos. Say, doth the dull soil
> Quarrel with the proud forests it hath fed,
> And feedeth still, more comely than itself?
> Can it deny the chiefdom of green groves?
> Or shall the tree be envious of the dove
> Because it cooeth, and hath snowy wings
> To wander wherewithal and find its joys?
> We are such forest-trees, and our fair boughs
> Have bred forth, not pale solitary doves,
> But eagles golden-feather'd, who do tower
> Above us in their beauty, and must reign
> In right thereof; for 'tis the eternal law
> That first in beauty should be first in might:
> Yea by that law, another race may drive
> Our conquerors to mourn as we do now.
> Have ye beheld the young God of the Seas,
> My dispossessor? Have ye seen his face?
> Have ye beheld his chariot, foam'd along
> By noble winged creatures he hath made?
> I saw him on the calmed waters scud,
> With such a glow of beauty in his eyes,
> That it enforc'd me to bid sad farewell
> To all my empire.

Thus speaks Oceanus. And the fallen deities, either convinced or in sullen anger, keep silence. At last one, of whom no one has thought, the goddess Clymene, breaks the long silence, speaking timidly among the fierce, with hectic lips and gentle glances:—

O Father, I am here the simplest voice,
And all my knowledge is that joy is gone,
And this thing woe crept in among our hearts.
There to remain for ever, as I fear:
I would not bode of evil, if I thought
So weak a creature could turn off the help
Which by just right should come of mighty Gods;
Yet let me tell my sorrow, let me tell
Of what I heard, and how it made me weep,
And know that we had parted from all hope.—
I stood upon a shore, a pleasant shore,
Where a sweet clime was breathed from a land
Of fragrance, quietness, and trees, and flowers.
Full of calm joy it was, as I of grief;
Too full of joy and soft delicious warmth;
So that I felt a movement in my heart
To chide, and to reproach that solitude
With songs of misery, music of our woes;
And sat me down, and took a mouthed shell
And murmured into it, and made melody—
O melody no more! for while I sang,
And with poor skill let pass into the breeze
The dull shell's echo, from a bowery strand
Just opposite, an island of the sea,
There came enchantment with the shifting wind,
That did both drown and keep alive my ears.
I threw my shell away upon the sand,
And a wave fill'd it, as my sense was fill'd
With that new blissful golden melody,
A living death was in each gush of sounds,
Each family of rapturous hurried notes,
That fell, one after one, yet all at once,
Like pearl beads dropping sudden from their
    string:
And then another, then another strain,
Each like a dove leaving its olive perch,
With music wing'd instead of silent plumes,
To hover round my head, and make me sick
Of joy and grief at once. Grief overcame,
And I was stopping up my frantic ears,
When, past all hindrance of my trembling hands,
A voice came sweeter, sweeter than all tune,
And still it cried, 'Apollo! young Apollo!
The morning-bright Apollo! young Apollo!'
I fled, it followed me, and cried 'Apollo!'

Keats has surpassed himself in this passage, which is as profound in thought as it is beautiful. It is not only a proof of the quality of his poetic gift, but the announcement of the appearance of a younger generation of poets in the field held by the poets of the Lake School and Scott. In the name of the reigning deities, the human intellect is too often condemned to inactivity and stagnation. If there is to be progress, a change of rulers is frequently called for. Wordsworth and Scott were mighty Titans whose glory paled when the younger generation appeared. Keats himself was the golden-feathered bird that rose high into the air above Wordsworth's leafy old oak. And Byron—was not he the new ocean god, who "troubled the waters" of passion with such power that the greatest literary genius of the day abdicated in his favour, assured that it was in vain to compete with him? And Shelley's melodies, intoxicatingly sweet, unprecedentedly daring—were they not borne on all the winds, and are they not still penetrating everywhere, though many, like Clymene, stop their ears and refrain as long as possible from listening to the new tones? The struggle is a vain one, for now on every side resounds the cry: "Apollo! morning-bright Apollo!"

The old gods, as in the poem, assumed different attitudes at this crisis in their fates. Scott, the noblest of them all, acknowledged his defeat by Byron with an amiable dignity which still further enhanced his reputation. Wordsworth retired to his Lakes, muttering an accusation of plagiarism. Southey poured forth volleys of abuse. Meanwhile the new, young gods mounted the thrones of the old, and round their heads shone the bright halo of the light that they gave forth.

Keats was the youngest of the young race of giants, and he had peculiar qualities and a peculiar domain of his own, into which none of the others intruded. He is one of the many examples of singularly delicate and refined organisms appearing in the most unlikely outward surroundings and developing almost unaided by circumstances. This youth who, dying at the age of twenty-six, has left behind him master-works which none who read them can forget, and whose name is immortalised in Shelley's *Adonais*, was the son of a London livery-stable keeper, and was bred an apothecary. Few of the elder literary celebrities knew him. Wordsworth, the only one among them on whom his eyes were steadily turned, and with more reverence than was felt by any of the other young men—even Wordsworth showed himself cold. At Haydon the painter's, one evening, when Wordsworth was present, Keats was induced to repeat to him the famous Hymn to Pan from the First Book of *Endymion*. The "iron-grey poet" heard it to the end, and then only remarked that it was "a pretty piece of paganism." And so, praise be to Keats, it is! Wordsworth, however, meant nothing flattering by the remark. Such was the verdict of the most influential member of the elder school of poetry. The elder school of criticism was distinctly adverse. Its verdict as harsh and scathing. Both the *Quarterly Review* and *Blackwood's Magazine* jeered foolishly at *Endymion*. The author was told that "it is a better and a wiser thing to be a starved apothecary than a starved poet," and was bidden "back to his gallipots." Calmly as the young poet writes of the ignominious treatment he received, there can be no doubt that the stingrankled deeply. It is most improbable that the report spread among Keats's acquaintances of the ruinous effect of these criticisms on his health, was, as is now maintained, entirely without foundation. He certainly was not, as Byron in *Don Juan* declares him to have been, killed by a savage article in the *Quarterly*; and his own utterances give ample proof of his profound contempt for these disparagements of his art and his personality; but his ambition was excessive, his susceptibility equally so, and his body contained the germs of a fatal disease; and it would be surprising if rancorous attacks from without had not affected an organism which was preyed upon from within by consuming passion and consuming disease.

John Keats was born in October 1795. At the age of nine he lost his father. His mother sent him to a good school; but she, too, to his inexpressible grief, died while he was still a boy. His appearance corresponded to the impression which his poetry makes on us. Whilst the feminine and ethereal Shelley had a slender, slightly-built, narrow-chested figure and a shrill voice, the heavier footed, more earth-bound Keats was deep-chested and broad-shouldered; his lower limbs were small in comparison with the upper; and he had a deep, grave voice. His small head was covered with thick brown curls; the eyes were large and of a dark, on occasion glowing, blue; the handsome mouth had a projecting lower lip, which gave the face a defiant and pugnacious expression. And as a matter of fact he was, as a boy, a perfect little terrier for resoluteness and pugnacity, and seemed much

more likely to distinguish himself in war than in literature. He early displayed great personal courage, and was an adept in all athletic exercises; just before he was attacked by consumption he thrashed an insolent butcher in a regular stand-up fight.

At the age of fifteen he left school, and was apprenticed by his relations to a clever surgeon-apothecary at Edmonton, with whom he remained till he was twenty, when he began, as a medical student, to walk the London hospitals. He soon, however, gave up medicine for literature, and lived for several years in close companionship with some of the rising young literary men and artists of the day. Then he was attacked by the disease which had carried off his mother and his younger brother. The absence of any prospect of earning a living, and the ever-increasing pressure of poverty, favoured its development, which was farther hastened by a violent and hopeless passion for a young Anglo-Indian lady—a passion only rendered hopeless by Keats's poverty and ill-health—his love being returned. His health obliged him to quit the neighbourhood of his beloved and take a journey to Italy, where he died.

Glancing over the non-literary part of Keats's life, we distinguish three facts of leading importance—his want of any real prospect of gaining a livelihood (he had thoughts of emigrating to South America, or applying for a post as surgeon on an Indiaman); the ardent and hopeless passion for the woman without whom life was worthless to him; and the wasting disease.

Miss Fanny Brawne was eighteen, five years younger than Keats, when he made her acquaintance in 1818. He and his friend, Brown, had settled at Hampstead, in a semi-detached house, the other half of which was occupied by Miss Brawne and her mother. The first six months after he fell in love were to Keats months of real happiness. In December 1818 he began *Hyperion*. In February 1819, the most fruitful month in his life, he wrote the *Ode to Psyche, The Eve of St Agnes*, and great part of *Hyperion*. And early in the spring, sitting under a plum-tree in the Brawnes' garden, he wrote his *Ode to the Nightingale*. In other words—his most beautiful poetry was written in the half year during which he took long walks with Fanny, and was still a healthy man. Unfortunately, it being possible for him to see his beloved every day, we have not a single love-letter dating from this, his short period of happiness. In July 1819 he wrote to her for the first time; and all the letters which he sent her from that date until the time of his death were published in 1878.

They are not melancholy to begin with. In one of the earliest he writes:

I want a brighter word than bright, a fairer word than fair;

and to some objection made by her he answers:

Why may I not speak of your Beauty, since without that I could never have lov'd you?— I cannot conceive any beginning of such love as I have for you but Beauty. There may be a sort of love for which, without the least sneer at it, I have the highest respect and can admire it in others; but it has not the richness, the bloom, the full form, the enchantment of love after my own heart.

Very soon, however, the jealousy which was to have such a wearing effect upon the lover appears in his letters. Again and again he exacts promises of eternal devotion. Though not yet ill, he has a vague presentiment that his end is not far off. He writes:

I have two luxuries to brood over in my walks; your Loveliness and the hour of my death. O that I could have possession of them both in the same minute!

Her letters had really only a depressing effect on him. He read them so often that each sentence assumed a distorted proportion; and they seemed to him now cold, now full of reproaches. He tortured first himself and then her with his suspicious irritableness and perversity; he would, for example, pass her door without going in, though he was longing to see her, and knew that his not appearing was a disappointment to her. There are a few perfectly happy, tender letters, dated October 1819. But in February 1820 commences a period of miserable excitement. He begins to spit blood, and "reads his death-warrant in its colour." After this the letters are short, some of them still playful and hopeful, others suspicious and violent in their jealousy—all brimming over with passion. Here is a fragment:

You know our situation—what hope is there if I should be recovered ever so soon—my very health will not suffer me to make any great exertion. I am recommended not even to read poetry, much less write it. I cannot say forget me—but I would mention that there are impossibilities in the world. No more of this. I am not strong enough to be weaned—take no notice of it in your goodnight.

During his apparent convalescence he is constantly begging her to come and show herself only for half a minute outside of the window through which he can see her, or to walk a little in the garden. Then he asks her not to come every day, because he cannot always bear to see her. But when, according to his wish, she does not come, he is restless and jealous.

As the end approaches, the letters become ever sadder and more distressing to read. The last of them are positively harrowing. He is as wild and helpless in his passionate despair as a child who believes himself forgotten. It is the mental death-struggle preceding the physical.

Fanny Brawne's tenderness for her lover never wavered. It is now evident that, as was only natural, this young girl with the touch of coquetry in her nature had no suspicion whatever of the gifts and powers of the poor consumptive youth who worshipped and tortured her. But she loved him for his own sake, and when, from the last letter, she learned in what a sad condition he really was, she and her mother would no longer leave him to the care of his friend, but took him into their own house in Wentworth Place, where he lived for the last month before he left for Italy. A stay in that country had been prescribed, as giving him a last chance of recovery.

The man to whom, in other circumstances, the prospect of seeing the country for which he had always longed, and whose gods he had awakened from the dead, would have given supreme happiness, now writes:

This journey to Italy wakes me at daylight every morning, and haunts me horribly. I shall endeavour to go, though it be with the sensation of marching up against a Battery.

On board ship he writes, referring to his attachment to Miss Brawne:

> Even if my body would recover of itself, this would prevent it. The very thing which I want to live most for will be a great occasion of my death. I cannot help it ... I wish for death every day and night to deliver me from these pains, and then I wish death away, for death would destroy even those pains which are better than nothing. Land and sea, weakness and decline, are great separators, but death is the great divorcer for ever ... I seldom think of my brother and sister in America. The thought of leaving Miss Brawne is beyond everything horrible—the sense of darkness coming over me—I eternally see her figure eternally vanishing."

And in another letter he writes:

> The persuasion that I shall see her no more will kill me. My dear Brown, I should have had her when I was in health, and I should have remained well. I can bear to die—I cannot bear to leave her. O God! God! God! Everything I have in my trunks that reminds me of her goes through me like a spear. The silk lining she put in my travelling cap scalds my head. My imagination is horribly vivid about her—I see her—I hear her. There is nothing in the world of sufficient interest to divert me from her for a moment ... I cannot say a word about Naples; I do not feel at all concerned in the thousand novelties around me. I am afraid to write to her—I should like her to know that I do not forget her. Oh, Brown, I have coals of fire in my breast. It surprises me that the human heart is capable of containing and bearing so much misery. Was I born for this end?

On the last day of November 1820, Keats wrote his last letter. His intimate old friend, Dr. Clark, a skilful physician, preserved his life till the end of the winter. While in Naples, Keats received a letter from his brother poet, Shelley, inviting him to come to Pisa, where he would be nursed and cared for in every way. But this invitation he did not accept. After several weeks of great suffering came rest and sleep, resignation and tranquillity. He desired that a letter from his beloved, which he had not dared to read, along with a purse and a letter which he had received from his sister, should be placed in his coffin; and that on his gravestone should be inscribed:

Here lies one whose name was writ in water.

The touch of Shelley's magic wand stiffened the water into crystal, and the name stands inscribed for all time.[1]

Keats's poetry is the most fragrant flower of English Naturalism. Before he appeared, this Naturalism had had a long period of vigorous growth. Its active principle had been evolved by Wordsworth, who developed it so methodically that he divided his poems into groups, corresponding to the different periods of human life and the different faculties of the soul. Coleridge provided it with the support of a philosophy of nature which had a strong resemblance to Schelling's. In Scott it assumes the highly successful form of a study of men, manners, and scenery, inspired by patriotism, by interest in history, and by a wonderful apprehension of the significance of race. Both in Moore and Keats it takes the form of gorgeous sensuousness, is the literary expression of the perceptions of beings whose sensitiveness to impressions of the beauty of the external world makes that of the average human being seem blunt and dull. But the sensuousness of Moore's poetry, which reveals itself artistically in his warm, bright colouring, is confined to the erotic domain, and is of a light and playful character. Keats's is full-blooded, serious sensuousness, by no means specially erotic, but all-embracing, and, in this its comprehensiveness, one of the most admirable developments of English Naturalism. This Naturalism led Wordsworth into one extreme, which has already been referred to; Keats it led into a different and more poetical one.

Keats was more of the artist than any of his English brother poets. He troubled himself less about principles than any of them. There is no groundwork of patriotism in his poetry as there is in Scott's and Moore's; no message of liberty, as in

---

[1] —*Fragment on Keats*: Shelley.
Death, the immortalising winter, flew
Athwart the stream—and time's printless
  torrent grew
A scroll of crystal, blazoning the name
Of Adonais.

Shelley's and Byron's; it is pure art, owing its origin to nothing but the power of imagination. It was one of his favourite sayings, that the poet should have no principles, no morality, *no self*. Why? Because the true poet enjoys both light and shade—has as much delight in conceiving an Iago as an Imogen. All poets who have forgotten themselves in the theme of their flights of fancy, have, when engaged in production, to the best of their ability banished their private peculiarities and preferences. Few have managed to make such a clean sweep as Keats of their personal hopes, enthusiasms, and principles. His study was, as one of his admirers has said, "a painter's studio with very little in it besides the easel."

Keats's poetical indifference to theories and principles was, however, in itself a theory and a principle—was the philosophy which has its foundation in poetic worship of nature. To the consistent pantheistic poet all forms, all shapes, all expressions of life on earth which engage the imagination, are precious, and all equally precious. Keats, as poet, recognises no truth of the kind that means improvement or exclusion; but he has an almost religious faith in imagination as the source of truth. In one of his letters he expresses himself thus:—

> I am certain of nothing but of the holiness of the heart's affections, and the truth of Imagination. What the Imagination seizes as Beauty must be Truth, whether it existed before or not;—for I have the same idea of all our passions as of Love: they are all, in their sublime, creative of essential Beauty … The Imagination may be compared to Adam's dream; he awoke and found it truth.

He enlarges on the difference between this kind of truth and the truth arrived at by consecutive reasoning, and concludes with an exclamation which is a key to the whole of his poetry:—

> However it may be, O for a life of sensations rather than of thoughts!

He led in great part a life of passive sensation, of pleasure and pain through the senses. Says Masson:

> Take a book of physiology and go over the so-called classes of sensations one by one—the sensations of the mere muscular states; the

sensations connected with such vital processes as circulation, alimentation, respiration, and electrical intercommunication with surrounding bodies; the sensations of taste; those of odour; those of hearing; and those of sight—and Keats will be found to have been unusually endowed in them all.

He had, for example, an extreme sensitiveness to the pleasures of the palate, and tried to heighten them by extraordinary stimulants. A friend tells us that he once saw Keats covering his tongue with cayenne pepper, that he might enjoy the delicious sensation of a draught of cold claret after it. He says himself in one of his letters:

> Talking of pleasure, this moment I was writing with one hand and with the other holding to my mouth a nectarine."

It is therefore not surprising that imagery drawn from the domain of the sense of taste is of frequent occurrence in Keats's poetry. In his deservedly famous *Ode to Melancholy* we are told that this goddess has her sovran shrine in the very temple of Delight—

> Though seen of none save him *whose strenuous tongue*
> *Can burst Joy's grape against his palate fine!*

And in one of his last sonnets he characteristically mentions "the palate of my mind losing its gust" as an indication of approaching death.

Naturally the senses of hearing and sight provided him with a much greater proportion of his imagery than the inferior, less noble senses. He had a musician's love of music and a painter's eye for variations of light and colour. And for all the different kinds of sound and smell and taste and sensations of touch, he possessed a store of words which any of the greatest poets might have envied. In short, he was by nature endowed with qualities which in combination, and in their full development, constituted supreme capacity to perceive and to reproduce all the beauty of nature.

To be able to reproduce it was from the very beginning his dream; and the man who affirmed that, except in the matter of art, he had no "opinions," expressed enthusiastic approval of the revolution of opinion in regard to the artificial, so-called classical, poetry of the eighteenth century, which had been brought about by Wordsworth and Coleridge. Spenser was Keats's idol, the classic poets were his aversion. In his poem, *Sleep and Poetry*, he has embodied an artistic confession of faith in language which could not well be more violent. After describing the old poetic triumphs of England, he exclaims:

> Could all this be forgotten? Yes, a schism
> Nurtured by foppery and barbarism
> Made great Apollo blush for this his land.
> Men were thought wise who could not
>   understand
> His glories; with a puling infant's force
> They sway'd about upon a rocking-horse
> And thought it Pegasus. Ah! Dismal-soul'd!
> The winds of heaven blew, the ocean roll'd
> Its gathering waves; ye felt it not. The blue
> Bared its eternal bosom, and the dew
> Of summer night collected still to make
> The morning precious; Beauty was awake!
> Why were *ye* not awake? .   .   .
> .   .   .   No, they went about.
> Holding a poor decrepit standard out,
> Mark'd with most flimsy mottoes, and, in large,
> The name of one Boileau!"

Long before the French assault upon this ancient, honoured name, Keats blows the war-trumpet! Théophile Gautier himself does not treat it with greater contempt.

It was probably the above passage, the energetic style of which reminds one of that picture of Kaulbach's in Munich, in which the artist of the rococo period is painted asleep with the lay-figure in his arms, which gave occasion to Byron's repeated thrusts at Keats as the traducer of Pope. For Keats never published a line against Pope; and when Countess Guiccioli, in her naïve work on Byron, refers to attacks which infuriated her lover, she is only repeating vague remarks she has heard. It is, however, highly probable that Keats included Pope among those whom he reproached with being deaf to the music of the waves and the winds, and with sleeping whilst the morning unfolded its beauties.

He himself was not of that company. If we examine the distinctive individuality of Keats's genius, we find its determining element to be the all-embracing sensuousness already alluded to. Read this stanza of the *Ode to a Nightingale*:—

> O, for a draught of vintage! that hath been
>   Cool'd a long age in the deep-delvèd earth,
> Tasting of Flora and the country green,
>   Dance, and Provençal song, and sun-burnt mirth!
> O for a beaker full of the warm South,
>   Full of the true, the blushful Hippocrene,
>   With beaded bubbles winking at the brim,
>   And purple-stainèd mouth;
> That I might drink, and leave the world unseen,
>   And with thee fade away into the forest dim.

And compare with it the following lines of *Endymion*:

> Taste these juicy pears,
> Sent me by sad Vertumnus;   .   .   .
> .   .   .   .   here is cream,
> Deepening to richness from a snowy gleam;
> Sweeter than that nurse Amalthea skimmed
> For the boy Jupiter: and here, undimmed
> By any touch, a bunch of blooming plums
> Ready to melt between an infant's gums.

The delicate, highly developed sense of taste is accompanied by an equally delicate and highly developed sense of touch and sense of smell. Read the passage in *Isabella*—a poem which, following Boccaccio, treats of the same theme as Hans Andersen's tale of the "Rose Fairy"—the passage which tells how the young girl took the head of her murdered lover from the grave:—

> Then in a silken scarf—sweet with the dews
>   Of precious flowers pluck'd in Araby,
> And divine liquids come with odorous ooze
>   Through the cold serpent pipe refreshfully,
> She wrapp'd it up.

and the lines in *Lamia*, describing the reception of the guests who come to take part in the wedding festivities:—

> When in an antechamber every guest
> Had felt the cold full sponge to pleasure press'd,
> By minist'ring slaves, upon his hands and feet,
> And fragrant oils with ceremony meet
> Pour'd on his hair, they all mov'd to the feast
> In white robes, and themselves in order placed
> Around the silken couches.

In one of the *Epistles* occurs a line, about a swan, into which is compressed an incredible amount of sensuous imagery. It is: "Kissing thy daily food from Naiads' pearly hands."

It is unnecessary to draw the reader's attention in detail to all the delicate charms of these fragments. Proceeding to the domain of the sense of sight, we find that it preeminently is Keats's territory, although it is never his eye alone which is impressed by his surroundings. Wordsworth's poetry of nature leads us out into the open air; following Keats, we enter a hot-house: a soft, moist warmth meets us; our eyes are attracted by brightly coloured flowers and juicy fruits; slender palms, amidst whose branches no rough wind ever blows, beckon gently with their huge fans. His *Ode to Autumn* is a characteristic specimen of his descriptions of nature. After telling of autumn's conspiracy with the sun

> to load and bless
> With fruit the vines that round the thatch-eaves
>   run;
> To bend with apples the moss'd cottage trees,
> And fill all fruit with ripeness to the core;
> To swell the gourd, and plump the hazel shells
> With a sweet kernel,

he with a masterly hand portrays autumn as a person:

> Who hath not seen thee oft amid thy store?
> Sometimes whoever seeks abroad may find
> Thee sitting careless on a granary floor,
> Thy hair soft-lifted by the winnowing wind:
> Or on a half-reap'd furrow sound asleep,
> Drowsed with the fume of poppies, while thy hook
> Spares the next swath and all its twinèd flowers.

It is impossible for Keats to name any conception or any thought without at once proceeding to represent it in a corporeal, plastic form. His numerous allegories have the same life and fire as if they were executed in stone by the best Italian artists of the sixteenth century. He says of Melancholy:

> She dwells with Beauty—Beauty that must die;
> And Joy, *whose hand is ever at his lips*
> *Bidding adieu.*

He says of Poetry:

> A drainless shower
> Of light is poesy; 'tis the supreme power;
> 'Tis *might half-slumb'ring on its own right arm.*

We see the scope of Keats's poetic powers steadily increasing. His point of departure, especially in some of the most beautiful of his smaller poems (for example, the *Ode to the Nightingale*), is the description of a purely physical condition, such as weariness, nervousness, thirst, languor, the drowsiness produced by opium. Upon this background of sensitiveness the sensuous pictures rise, distinct and round, like the reliefs upon a shield. The word "welded" comes involuntarily to one's lips when one thinks of Keats's pictures. There is something firm and finished about them, as if they were welded on a metal plate.

Observe how the figures rise gradually into relief in the following stanzas, the first and third of the beautiful *Ode to Indolence*:

> One morn before me were three figures seen
>   With bowed necks and joined hands, side-faced;
> And one behind the other stepped serene,
>   In placid sandals, and in white robes graced;
>   They passed like figures on a marble urn,
>   When shifted round to see the other side;
> They came again; as when the urn once more
>   Is shifted round, the first green shades return,
>   And they were strange to me, as may betide
> With vases, to one deep in Phidian lore.
> .   .   .   .
> A third time passed they by, and, passing, turned
>   Each one the face a moment whiles to me;
> Then faded, and to follow them I burned
>   And ached for wings, because I knew the three;
>   The first was a fair maid, and Love her name;
>   The second was Ambition, pale of cheek,
> And ever watchful, with fatigued eye;
>   The last, whom I love more, the more of blame
>   Is heaped upon her, maiden most unmeek—
> I knew to be my demon, Poesy.

But not until he wrote the two completed books of *Hyperion* did Keats attain to absolute mastery over his artistic material, and realise the ideal of sensuous plasticity which was ever before his eyes. In this work the relief has been superseded by the statue; and they are statues, these, which impress us with the feeling that Michael Angelo's chisel must have played a part in their production. Granted that the influence of Milton is clearly perceptible—there is more than Milton here. The nature of the subject demanded the colossal.

We are told of the goddess Thea:

By her in stature the tall Amazon
Had stood a pigmy's height; she would have ta'en
Achilles by the hair and bent his neck;
Or with a finger stay'd Ixion's wheel.

And read this description of the cavern where the Titans are assembled after their fall:—

It was a den where no insulting light
Could glimmer on their tears; where their own
    groans
They felt, but heard not, for the solid roar
Of thunderous waterfalls and torrents hoarse,
Pouring a constant bulk, uncertain where.
Crag jutting forth to crag, and rocks that seem'd
Ever as if just rising from a sleep,
Forehead to forehead held their monstrous
    horns;
And thus in thousand hugest phantasies
Made a fit roofing to this nest of woe.
Instead of thrones, hard flint they sat upon,
Couches of rugged stone, and slaty ridge
Stubborn'd with iron. All were not assembled:
Some chain'd in torture, and some wandering.
Cæus, and Gyges, and Briareüs,
Typhon, and Dolor, and Porphyrion,
With many more, the brawniest in assault,
Were pent in regions of laborious breath;
Dungeon'd in opaque element, to keep
Their clenchèd teeth still clench'd, and all their
    limbs
Locked up like veins of metal, crampt and screw'd;
Without a motion, save of their big hearts
Heaving in pain, and horribly convuls'd
With sanguine feverous boiling gurge of pulse.

Byron, who had been very severe in his criticism of Keats's previous works, said, and said truly, of *Hyperion*:

It seems actually inspired by the Titans, and is as sublime as Æschylus.

The specimens of his poetry here quoted afford sufficient proof of Keats's imaginative power. It is to it, and not to his melodies, sweet as they are, that he owes his rank among English poets.[2] The purely artistic character of his verse makes of him the connecting link between the conservative and the progressive poets. He has a distinct bias in the direction of progress. Of this his enthusiastic friendship for the Radical editor of the *Examiner*, Leigh Hunt, is a striking proof. He felt what he wrote when, in his indignation at the proceedings of the Liverpool-Castlereagh ministry, he exclaimed (in his poem *To Hope*):

O, let me see our land retain her soul,
    Her pride, her freedom; and not freedom's shade!

And William Tell, Wallace, and, chief of all, Kosciuszko, are named again and again in his verse with the profoundest admiration. What he might have developed into if he had reached maturity, it is impossible to tell. When he wrote his last poems he was still but a child, ignorant of the world.

And it must not be forgotten that while he wrote them he was enduring great physical suffering, and mental anxiety amounting to torture. Perhaps it is for this very reason they are so beautiful. Let the artist keep his private life long enough out of his work—let him, like Keats, hardly make any allusion in his poetry to his most absorbing passion—and no work will have such life, such colour, such divine fire as that executed whilst he not only wrought, but lived and suffered. Neither the precariousness of Keats's circumstances, nor his hopeless state of health, nor his passion for Fanny Brawne, set any distinct mark on his poetry; but from all this poison for himself he drew nourishment for it.

He sank into his early grave, but hardly had the earth closed over him before he rose again from the dead in Shelley's great elegy. He ceased to exist as Keats; he was transformed into a myth, into Adonais, into the beloved of all the Muses and the elements; and henceforward he had, as it were, a double existence in the consciousness of the age.

---

[2] Note the melodiousness of the Fairy Song:
    Shed no tear! O shed no tear!
    The flower will bloom another year.
    Weep no more! O weep no more!
    Young buds sleep in the root's white core, &c.

He lives, he wakes—'tis Death is dead, not he;
  Mourn not for Adonais .   .   .

He is made one with Nature. There is heard
  His voice in all her music, from the moan
Of thunder to the song of night's sweet bird …

He is a portion of the loveliness
  Which once he made more lovely. He doth bear
His part, while the One Spirit's plastic stress
  Sweeps through the dull dense world, compelling
    there
  All new successions to the forms they wear …

The inheritors of unfulfilled renown
  Rose from their thrones, built beyond mortal
    thought,
Far in the unapparent. Chatterton
  Rose pale, his solemn agony had not
  Yet faded from him; Sidney, as he fought,
And as he fell, and as he lived and loved,
  Sublimely mild, a spirit without spot,
Arose   .   .   .   .   .

And many more, whose names on earth are dark,
  But whose transmitted effluence cannot die
So long as fire outlives the parent spark,
  Rose, robed in dazzling immortality.
    'Thou art become as one of us,' they cry;
'It was for thee yon kingless sphere has long
  Swung blind in unascended majesty,
  Silent alone amid an heaven of song.
Assume thy winged throne, thou Vesper of our throng![3]

We search the history of literature in vain for a parallel to this elegy. It is instant transfiguration after death—a poetic transfiguration of a purely naturalistic and purely human kind. To Shelley, Keats's true apotheosis was what he expresses in the words: "He is made one with Nature."

---

[3] Shelley: *Adonais.*

SHELLEY

XVI

RADICAL NATURALISM

IF IN THE YEAR 1820, ANY RESPECTABLE, well-educated Englishman had been asked: "Who is Shelley?" he would undoubtedly, if he could answer the question at all, have replied: "He is said to be a bad poet with shocking principles and a worse than doubtful character. The *Quarterly Review*, which is not given to defamation, says that he himself is distinguished by 'low pride, cold selfishness, and unmanly cruelty' and his poetry by its frequent and total want of meaning.' He has lately published a poem called *Prometheus Unbound*, the verse of which the same review calls 'drivelling prose run mad.' And the press is unanimous in this opinion. The *Literary Gazette* writes that, if it were not assured to the contrary, it would take it for granted that the author of *Prometheus Unbound* was a lunatic—as his principles are ludicrously wicked, and his poetry is a mélange of nonsense, cockneyism, poverty, and pedantry. It calls the work in question 'the stupid trash of this delirious dreamer.'"

And it is quite possible that our Englishman would have added, in an undertone: "There are very bad reports in circulation about Shelley. The *Literary Gazette*, which is always specially severe on the enemies of religion, hints at incest. It declares that 'to such a man it would be a matter of perfect indifference to rob a confiding father of his daughters, and incestuously to live with all the branches of a family whose morals were ruined by the damned sophistry of the seducer.' These expressions may be too strong, but it is hardly credible that they are entirely undeserved; for *Blackwood's Magazine*, the only periodical which has been at all favourable to Shelley, writes of his *Prometheus*:

It seems impossible that there can exist a more pestiferous mixture of blasphemy, sedition, and sensuality.

And you may possibly have heard Theodore Hook's witty saying:

Prometheus Unbound—it is well named: who would bind it?

And if, two years later, when this harshly reviewed poet was already dead, the same curious inquirer had applied to the publisher for information as to the saleableness of the fiercely attacked works, the latter would quite certainly have complained of them as a bad business speculation, and told his questioner that, during Shelley's lifetime, not a hundred copies of any of his works, except *Queen Mab* and *The Cenci*, had been sold, and that, as far as *Adonais* and *Epipsychidion* were concerned, ten would be nearer the number.

If any one were to ask now: Who was Shelley? what a different answer would be given! But today there is no one in England who would ask.

It was on the 4th of August 1792 that England's greatest lyric poet was born. On the same day on which, in Paris, the leaders of the Revolution—Santerre, Camille Desmoulins, and others—were meeting in a house on the Boulevards to make the arrangements which resulted, a few days later, in the fall of monarchy in France, there came into the world at Field Place, in the English county of Sussex, a pretty little boy with deep blue eyes, whose life was to be of greater and more enduring significance in the emancipation of the human mind than all that happened in France in August 1792. Not quite thirty years later his name—Percy Bysshe Shelley—was carved upon the stone in the Protestant cemetery in Rome under which his ashes lie; and below the name are engraved the words: *Cor cordium*.

Cor cordium, heart of hearts—such was the simple inscription in which Shelley's young wife summed up his character; and they are the truest, profoundest words she could have chosen.

P. B. SHELLEY

The Shelleys are an ancient and honourable family. The poet's father, Sir Timothy Shelley, was a wealthy landowner. He was a narrow-minded man, a supporter of the existing, for the simple reason that it existed. But revolt against rule and convention was hereditary in Shelley's family, as wildness and violence of temper were in Byron's. Percy's grandfather, a strange, restless man, eloped with two of his three wives; and two of his daughters in their turn eloped. Of these incidents we are reminded by similar occurrences in the life of the grandson—just as many an action of Byron's reminds us of the sum of untamed and reckless passionateness which was his indisputable inheritance from father and mother. Unconventionality, revolt against hard and fast rule, was, however, but an outward and comparatively unimportant part of Shelley's character and life. It was only a sign of the alert receptivity and the keen sensitiveness, the early development of which strikes every student of his biographies. At school, ill-used himself, he rebels against the ill-treatment to which, according to the prevalent English custom, the weaker and younger boys were subjected by the older boys, and in this case also by the masters. Shelley seems to have been in a very special manner the victim of this species of brutality, just as he was in later life of many other species; there was a natural antipathy between him and everything base and stupid and foul, and he never entered into a compromise with any one or any thing of this nature.

We gain a distinct idea of what his impressions were on his entrance into life, from a fragment found after his death upon a scrap of paper:—

Alas! this is not what I thought life was.
    I knew that there were crimes and evil men,
Misery and hate; nor did I hope to pass,
    Untouched by suffering, through the rugged glen.
In mine own heart I saw as in a glass
The hearts of others.

He wrought for his soul, he tells us, "a linked armour of calm steadfastness." But passionate indignation had preceded this mood of quiet resistance; and the soul which he armed with steadfastness was too enthusiastic and ardent not to lay plans of attack behind its defences.

In the introduction to the *Revolt of Islam*, he recalls "the hour which burst his spirit's sleep":—

A fresh May-dawn it was,
When I walked forth upon the glittering grass,
And wept, I knew not why: until there rose
From the near schoolroom voices that, alas!
Were but one echo from a world of woes—
The harsh and grating strife of tyrants and of foes.

And then I clasped my hands, and looked around:
But none was near to mock my streaming eyes,
Which poured their warm drops on the sunny ground.
So, without shame, I spake: 'I will be wise,
And just, and free, and mild, if in me lies
Such power; for I grow weary to behold
The selfish and the strong still tyrannise
Without reproach or check.' I then controlled
My tears, my heart grew calm, and I was meek and bold.

The generation which was born at the same time and under the same planet as the first French Republic was precocious in its criticism of all traditional beliefs and conventions. Shelley, who at school saw tyranny and feigned piety attendant on one another, and who became acquainted at a very early age with the writings of the French Encyclopædists and of Hume, Godwin, and other English freethinkers, brooded deeply, long before he was grown up, on the history, the destiny, and the errors of the human race. His thoughts were the thoughts of an immature youth, but their spirit was the spirit of liberty, as understood by the eighteenth century.

What his comrades remembered about him in later years was his defiant attitude towards authority, more particularly a habit he had of "cursing his father and the king." He went among the boys by the name of "mad Shelley," and "Shelley the atheist." Thus early was the opprobrious word applied to him which was to be coupled with his name all his life, and serve as a pretext for abuse and defamation.

It is unnecessary to dwell upon those events in Shelley's life of which every one who has heard his name has at least a superficial knowledge. We need merely recall to mind the fact that, as the undergraduate of eighteen, he had the curious habit of writing down his heresies on such subjects as God, government, and society, in the form of letters, which he sent to people personally unknown to him, with the request that they would refute his theories and provide him with the proofs against his arguments which he himself was unable to find; that, out of these letters, which consisted chiefly of extracts from the works of Hume and the French materialists, grew a little anonymous pamphlet (no longer in existence) which was entitled *The Necessity of Atheism* and ended with a Q.E.D.; and that Shelley, in the childish hope of exercising a reforming influence on the spirit of his age, sent a copy of this pamphlet to the Bench of Bishops. What followed is equally well known. Shelley, denounced as the author, was not only expelled from the University, but from his father's house.

No one nowadays considers that any serious scientific conviction, in whatever manner it may be expressed, should bring disgrace and punishment upon its exponent; and Shelley's punishment appears to us doubly unreasonable when we discover that in his pamphlet (the substance of which he reprinted in the notes to *Queen Mab*) he is no more an atheist than, for example, our Oersted[4] is in his well-known work, *The Spirit in Nature*. He has not yet arrived at any logical and consistent theory of life; he is only clear on the one main point, that he is not, and never can become, an adherent of any so-called revealed religion. The materialistic impressions received from the books he has read are blent in his mind with the ardent pantheism which distinguished him to the last. When Trelawny asked him in 1822, the year in which he died: Why do you call yourself an atheist? Shelley replied:

I used the name to express my abhorrence of superstition; I took up the word, as a knight took up the gauntlet, in defiance of injustice.

Shelley had grown up tall and slight, narrow-chested, his features small and not regular except the mouth, which was beautiful, clever, and fascinating; there was a feminine and almost seraphic look in the eyes, and the whole face was distinguished by an infinite play of expression. He sometimes looked the age he was—nineteen, sometimes as if he were forty. In the course of the ten remaining years of his life he became more manly in appearance, but still often struck people as boyish and feminine looking—witness Trelawny's surprise at his first meeting with Shelley:

Was it possible this mild-looking beardless boy could be the veritable monster at war with all the world, and denounced by the rival sages of our literature as the founder of a Satanic school?

His countenance assumed every expression—earnest, joyful, touchingly sorrowful, listlessly weary; but what it suggested most frequently in later years was promptitude and decision. He often expressed in his face the feeling he put into words in his poem *To Edward Williams*:

Of hatred I am proud—with scorn content;
　　Indifference, that once hurt me, now is grown
　　　　Itself indifferent.

To all this we may add, employing words used by a friend of his youth, that he looked "preternaturally intelligent"; and that Mulready, a distinguished painter of the day, said it was simply impossible to paint Shelley's portrait—he was "too beautiful."

It is, then, as a youth of this nature—excitable as a poet, brave as a hero, gentle as a woman, blushing and shy as a young girl, swift and light as Shakespeare's Ariel—that we must think of Shelley going out and in among his friends. Mrs. Williams said of him: "He comes and goes like a spirit, no one knows when or where."

His health was extremely delicate all his life, and would probably have given way altogether if he had not rigidly adhered to the simplest diet. About 1812 he adopted vegetarianism, with doubtful benefit. He was of a consumptive habit and subject to nervous and spasmodic attacks, which were sometimes so violent that he rolled on the floor in agony, and had recourse to opium to dull the pain; when he had his worst attacks he would not let the opium bottle out of his hand. When he was visiting the London hospitals and studying medicine with the aim of being able to assist the poor, he himself became seriously ill, and an eminent physician prophesied that he would die of consumption. But his lungs completely righted themselves some years later. In 1817, in attending some of the poor in their cottages, he caught a bad attack of ophthalmia; and he had a relapse of the same malady at the end of the year, and another in 1821, each time severe enough to prevent his reading.

---

[4] Hans Christian Ørsted.

The lofty philanthropy which to him was a religion, demanded many offerings. He displayed it wherever he went. When he was living at Marlow, in anything but affluent circumstances, he made all the poor of the neighbourhood his pensioners; they came to his house every week for their allowances, and he went to them when they were kept at home by sickness. One day he appeared barefooted at the house of a neighbour; he had given away his shoes to a poor woman. Of his own accord, almost immediately after his expulsion from Oxford, he gave up, for the benefit of his sisters, his claim to the greater part of his father's estate. At the time when he was enjoying an income of about £1000 a year, he spent most of it in assisting others, especially poor men of letters, whose debts he paid, and to whom he showed generosity almost unjustifiable in a man of his means.

The story of his first marriage is as follows. Exaggerated and mistaken chivalry led him at the age of nineteen to elope with a schoolgirl of sixteen, named Harriet Westbrook, who was very much in love with him, and had complained bitterly to him of her father's ill-treatment of her (he had forbidden her to love Shelley, and tried to compel her to go to school!). Shelley, after various meetings with her, made his plans, carried her off to Scotland, and married her in Edinburgh. The censure of public opinion fell most severely on the poet for this behaviour; but W. M. Rossetti's remark is very much to the point, namely, that it would be interesting to know "what percentage of faultlessly Christian young heirs of opulent baronets would have acted like the atheist Shelley, and married a retired hotel-keeper's daughter offering herself as a mistress." The hasty union, contracted without any proper consideration, proved an unhappy one; and it was dissolved when, in 1814, Shelley made the acquaintance of Mary Wollstonecraft Godwin, then in her seventeenth year, and was inspired by her with an irresistible passion. Mary Godwin, the daughter of Mary Wollstonecraft, the first famous pleader for the emancipation of woman, and of William Godwin, the free-thinking author of the works which had had such an influence on Shelley in his earliest youth, gave him her love frankly and freely, and in so doing acted strictly according to her own code of right. The young couple's theories of marriage, which were too ideal not to be regarded as vile by the vile, were also too impracticable. Although in their eyes mutual love alone, and not any ecclesiastical or civil formality, constituted the sacred marriage tie, they nevertheless for practical reasons, and especially for the sake of their children, went through the customary marriage ceremony in 1816, after the suicide of Shelley's first wife. Before this they had been twice abroad, first on a short tour, great part of which was taken on foot, and then for a longer period of travel, during which they met Byron. Shelley's name was, accordingly, coupled with Byron's, and the English press attacked them both with the utmost fury, going so far as to put a shameful interpretation on their noble and manly friendship.

Southey found occasion for a perfect explosion of abuse in the circumstance, insignificant and harmless enough, that Shelley had written in the album kept for visitors at the Chartreuse at Montanvert in the valley of Chamounix, below a number of pious platitudes about "Nature and Nature's God," a misspelled line in Greek hexameter said:

εἰμι φιλάνθρωπος δημωκράτικος τ' ἄθεός τε[5]
PERCY B. SHELLEY.

The well-known outburst against Lord Byron, which has been already touched on, has this utterance as its point of departure.

Such is, given in a few words, the overture to Shelley's life and poetry.

Cor cordium was his rightful appellation—for what he understood and felt was the innermost heart of things, their soul and spirit; and the feelings to which he gave expression were those inmost feelings, for which words seem too coarse, and which find vent only in music or in such verse as his, which is musical as richly harmonised melodies.

The suppressed melancholy of Shelley's lyrics sometimes reminds us of Shakespeare. The little spinning song in *The Cenci*, for example, recalls Amiens' song in *As You like It* or the songs of Desdemona and Ophelia.

But where Shelley is most himself he surpasses Shakespeare in delicacy; and there is no other poet with whom he can be compared; no one surpasses him. The short poems of 1821 and 1822 are, one may venture to say, the most exquisite in the English language.

---

[5] *I am a friend of humanity, a friend of the people and a denier of God.*

Take as a specimen the little poem entitled *A Dirge*:—

Rough wind that moanest loud
  Grief too sad for song;
Wild wind when sullen cloud
  Knells all the night long;
Sad storm whose tears are vain,
Bare woods whose branches stain.
Deep caves and dreary main,
  Wail for the world's wrong!

And wondrous in melody and restraint of expression is a verse like this:—

One word is too often profaned
  For me to profane it;
One feeling too falsely disdained
  For thee to disdain it;
One hope is too like despair
  For prudence to smother;
And pity from thee more dear
  Than that from another.

The words are few, and there is nothing remarkable in the rhythm, yet there is not a line that could have come from any pen but Shelley's.

In these short poems we are clearly conscious of the poet's melancholy, a melancholy which in his longer works is veiled, or else overpowered by his belief in a bright future, his faith in the progress of the human race. The inmost recesses of his own being were penetrated by a sadness produced by the feeling of the mutability of everything, and by early experience of the manner in which feeling leads astray, love disappoints, and life deceives.

He has given imperishable expression to the feeling of mutability:—

The flower that smiles today
  To-morrow dies:
All that we wish to stay
  Tempts and then flies.
What is this world's delight?
Lightning that mocks the night.
  Brief even as bright.

Virtue, how frail it is!
  Friendship how rare!
Love, how it sells poor bliss
  For proud despair!
But we, though soon they fall,
Survive their joy, and all
  Which ours we call.

Whilst skies are blue and bright,
  Whilst flowers are gay,
Whilst eyes that change ere night
  Make glad the day,
Whilst yet the calm hours creep,
Dream thou—and from thy sleep
  Then wake to weep.

The first verse indicates the transitoriness of all earthly beauty and happiness; the second, the suffering that lies concealed in the very happiness; and the third is an exhortation to enjoy the dream of happiness as long as possible.

A mood of like nature has found expression in the incomparable poem which bears the simple title, *Lines*. This poem Shelley could not have written unless one after another of his own fond beliefs had evaporated, unless his passions for Harriet, for Mary, for Emilia Viviani, had ended in a sorrowful awakening. Yet it bears no trace of being a personal confession. It is an impassioned proclamation of the universal laws of life, first softly hummed, and then sung in a voice which has never had its equal.

When the lamp is shattered,
The light in the dust lies dead;
  When the cloud is scattered,
The rainbow's glory is shed;
  When the lute is broken,
Sweet notes are remembered not;
  When the lips have spoken,
Loved accents are soon forgot.

The lines on the human heart in the third verse are as condensed as a couplet of Pope's and as melodious as bars of Beethoven:—

O, Love, who bewailest
The frailty of all things here,
  Why chose you the frailest
For your cradle, your home, and your bier?

And the poem ends with this prophecy, in which we can hear the passions that have taken possession of the heart taking their wild will with it:—

Its passions will rock thee,
As the storms rock the ravens on high:
   Bright reason will mock thee,
Like the sun from a wintry sky.
   From thy nest every rafter
Will rot, and thine eagle home
   Leave thee naked to laughter
When leaves fall and cold winds come.

A certain characteristic of Shelley, one which readers who know him only from anthologies will at once cite as his chief characteristic, seems to be strongly at variance with this unexampled personal intensity. I refer to the well-known fact that the most famous of his lyric poems are inspired by subjects outside of the emotional life, nay, outside of the world of man altogether; they treat of the cloud and the gale, of the life of the elements, of the marvellous freedom and stormy strength of wind and water. They are meteorological and cosmical poems. Yet there is no real contradiction in the most intimately emotional of lyric poets being, to all appearance, the most occupied with externals. We find the reason for it given by Shelley himself in a short essay *On Love*. He describes the essence of love as an irresistible craving for sympathy:

If we reason, we would be understood; if we imagine, we would that the airy children of our brain were born anew within another's; if we feel, we would that another's nerves should vibrate to our own, that lips of motionless ice should not reply to lips quivering and burning with the heart's best blood. This is Love … The meeting with an understanding capable of clearly estimating our own; an imagination which should enter into and seize upon the subtle and delicate peculiarities which we have delighted to cherish and unfold in secret … this is the invisible and unattainable point to which Love tends … Hence in solitude, or in that deserted state when we are surrounded by human beings, and yet they sympathise not with us, we love the flowers, the grass, the waters, and the sky… . There is eloquence in the tongueless wind, and a melody in the flowing brooks which bring tears of mysterious tenderness to the eyes, like the voice of one beloved singing to you alone.

In a note on *The Witch of Atlas*, Mrs. Shelley, too, writes that it was the certainty of neither being able to arouse the sympathy nor win the approbation of his countrymen, in combination with a shrinking from opening the wounds of his own heart by portraying human passion, which led her husband to seek forgetfulness in the airiest flights of fancy.

It was this very craving for a sympathy which his fellow-creatures refused him, that made his feeling for nature an ardent desire, and gave it its wonderful originality. Such a thing was unknown in English poetry. The stiff, artificial school of Pope had been superseded by the Lake School. Pope had perfumed the air with affectation; the Lake School had thrown open the windows and let in the fresh air of the mountains and the sea. But Wordsworth's love of nature was passionless, whatever he may say to the contrary in *Tintern Abbey*. Nature was to him an invigorator and a suggester of Protestant reflections. That meanest flower which gave him thoughts that often lay too deep for tears, he put into his buttonhole as an ornament, and looked at sometimes in a calmly dignified manner, revolving a simile. Shelley flees to nature for refuge when men shut their doors upon him. He does not, like others, feel it to be something entirely outside of himself— cold, or indifferent, or cruel. Its stony calm where man's woe and weal are concerned, its divine impassibility as regards our life and death, our short triumphs and long sufferings, are to him benevolence in comparison with man's stupidity and brutality. In *Peter Bell the Third* he jeers at Wordsworth because in the latter's love of nature it was "his drift to be a kind of moral eunuch"; he himself loves her like an ardent lover; he has pursued her most secret steps like her shadow; his pulse beats in mysterious sympathy with hers. He himself, like his Alastor, resembles "the Spirit of Wind, with lightning eyes and eager breath, and feet disturbing not the drifted snow."

He calls animals and plants his beloved brothers and sisters, and compares himself, with his keen susceptibility and his trembling sensitiveness, to the chameleon and the sensitive plant. In one of his poems he writes of the chameleons, which live on light and air, as the poet does on love and fame, and which change their hue with the light twenty times a day; and compares the life led by the poet on this cold earth with that which chameleons might lead if they were hidden from their birth in a cave beneath the sea. And in one of the most famous of all he tells how:

A Sensitive Plant in a garden grew;
And the young winds fed it with silver dew;
And it opened its fan-like leaves to the light,
And closed them beneath the kisses of night.
.   .   .   .

(And) each (flower) was interpenetrated
With the light and the odour its neighbour shed,
Like young lovers whom youth and love make dear.
Wrapped and filled by their mutual atmosphere.

But the Sensitive Plant, which could give small fruit
Of the love which it felt from the leaf to the root,
Received more than all; it loved more than ever,
Where none wanted but it, could belong to the giver:—

For the Sensitive Plant has no bright flower;
Radiance and odour are not its dower;
It loves even like Love—its deep heart is full;
It desires what it has not, the beautiful.

Even more characteristically, even more personally, does Shelley's inmost feeling, his heart's heart, such as it became after hard fate had set its stamp upon it, express itself in the beautiful elegy on Keats, which was written in a frame of burning indignation produced by the base and rancorous attack in the *Quarterly Review*. He is describing how all the poets of the day come to weep over their brother's bier:—

Midst others of less note came one frail form,
    A phantom among men, companionless
As the last cloud of an expiring storm
    Whose thunder is its knell. He, as I guess,
    Had gazed on Nature's naked loveliness
Actæon-like; and now he tied astray
    With feeble steps o'er the world's wilderness,
    And his own thoughts along that rugged way
Pursued like raging hounds their father and their prey.

A pard-like Spirit beautiful and swift—
    A love in desolation masked—a power
Girt round with weakness; it can scarce uplift
    The weight of the superincumbent hour.
    It is a dying lamp, a falling shower,
A breaking billow;—even whilst we speak
    Is it not broken? On the withering flower
The killing sun smiles brightly: on a cheek
The life can burn in blood even while the heart may
    break.

His head was bound with pansies overblown,
    And faded violets, white and pied and blue;
And a light spear topped with a cypress cone,
    Round whose rude shaft dark ivy-tresses grew
    Yet dripping with the forest's noonday dew,
Vibrated, as the ever-beating heart
    Shook the weak hand that grasped it. Of that crew
He came the last, neglected and apart;
A herd-abandoned deer struck by the hunter's dart.

All stood aloof, and at his partial moan
    Smiled through their tears. Well knew that gentle
    band
Who in another's fate now wept his own.
    As in the accents of an unknown land
    He sang new sorrow, sad Urania scanned
The Stranger's mien, and murmured, 'Who art thou?'
    He answered not, but with a sudden hand
Made bare his branded and ensanguined brow,
Which was like Cain's or Christ's—Oh I that it should
    be so."

Shelley here compares himself to Actæon, whom the sight of Nature's naked loveliness drove distracted. It is plain that the strength of his strong will was required to keep this man with the fragile, delicate body from positive destruction by the visions and apparitions of his imagination. He often felt as if they were more than his brain could bear; and when he then, an exile in a foreign land, sought alleviation in solitude, he experienced such impressions of nature as that which is preserved in the entrancing *Stanzas Written in Dejection near Naples*, stanzas which contain the very essence of Shelley's poetry. He does not describe the landscape. He never does describe. It is not the outward forms and colours of things which he shows us, but that to which he is extraordinarily alive, what we have called their spirit and soul.

One or two touches, and the Bay is before us:—

The sun is warm, the sky is clear,
    The waves are dancing fast and bright;
Blue isles and snowy mountains wear
    The purple noon's transparent might.

The waves break upon the shore "like light dissolved, in star-showers thrown." The lightning of the noontide ocean is flashing, and a tone arises from its measured motion. "How sweet," cries the poet, "did any heart now share in my emotion!"

Alas! I have nor hope nor health,
　　Nor peace within nor calm around;
Nor that content, surpassing wealth,
　　The sage in meditation found,
　　And walked with inward glory crowned;
Nor fame nor power nor love, nor leisure.
　　Others I see whom these surround—
Smiling they live, and call life pleasure;—
To me that cup has been dealt in another measure.

Yet now despair itself is mild,
　　Even as the winds and waters are;
I could lie down like a tired child,
　　And weep away the life of care
　　Which I have borne and yet must bear—
Till death like sleep might steal on me;
　　And I might feel in the warm air
My cheek grow cold, and hear the sea
Breathe o'er my dying brain its last monotony.

Some might lament that I were cold,
　　As I when this sweet day is gone,
Which my lost heart, too soon grown old,
　　Insults with this untimely moan.
　　They might lament—for I am one
Whom men love not, and yet regret;
　　Unlike this day, which, when the sun
Shall on its stainless glory set,
Will linger, though enjoyed, like joy in memory yet.

The man over whose dying brain cruel waves were so soon to close, feels, with a gentle mournfulness, his being dissolve into the beneficent elements of nature, and compares his last breath to that of the beautiful southern summer day. He did not, like Byron, love nature only in its agitated, wild moments; simple of heart himself, he loved its simplicity, its holy calm.

But this is not his most characteristic feature. Himself of the race of Titans and giants, he loves the Titanic and gigantic beauty of nature—his manner of doing so again differing entirely from Byron's. It is not the tangible, easily accessible poetry of nature, that of the flowers of the field or the trees of the forest, which inspires him at his highest. No! the finest inspirations of his great spirit are received from the grand and the distant, from the forceful motions of the sea and the air and the dance of the spheres in the firmament of heaven. In this familiarity with the great phenomena and the great vicissitudes of nature Shelley resembles Byron, but he resembles him as a fair genius resembles a

dark, as Ariel resembles Lucifer the Son of the Morning.

The poetry of the sea was to Byron the poetry of shipwreck, of the raging hurricane, of the insatiable cry of the waves for prey; to him the poetry of the sky lay in the howling of the storm, the roaring of the thunder, the crackle of the lightning. It is nature as the annihilator that he lives with and glories in. The famous passage in the Fourth Canto of *Childe Harold*, beginning: "Roll on, thou deep and dark blue Ocean, roll!" is a jubilant record of the sea's exploits in sweeping argosies from its surface and sinking empires into its depths. It boasts that nothing longer-lived than a bubble tells where man has gone down. The passage is like a prelude to the magnificent Deluge scene which is entitled *Heaven and Earth*, and which is a glorification of the lust of annihilation.[6]

After such verse read Shelley's famous poem, *The Cloud*. In it we hear all the elementary forces of nature playing and jesting, with the gaiety of giants, benevolent giants, who joy in pouring bounteous gifts upon the earth. What freshness in the lines:

I bring fresh showers for the thirsty flowers
　　From the seas and the streams;
I bear light shade for the leaves when laid
　　In their noonday dreams.

How wanton is the cloud when it sings:

I wield the flail of the lashing hail
　　And whiten the green plains under;
And then again I dissolve it in rain,
　　And laugh as I pass in thunder,
I sift the snow on the mountains below,
　　And their great pines groan aghast;
And all the night 'tis my pillow white,
　　While I sleep in the arms of the Blast.

And

The volcanoes are dim, and the stars reel and swim,
When the Whirlwinds my banner unfurl.

How proud when it shouts:

---

[6] Swinburne, who in his masterly little essay on Byron points out that Byron and Shelley were engrossed by the same natural phenomena, does not note the difference which existed along with the similarity.

The sanguine Sunrise, with his meteor eyes,
    And his burning plumes outspread,
Leaps on the back of my sailing rack,
    When the morning star shines dead.

What calm is in this:

And, when Sunset may breathe, from the lit sea
    beneath,
    Its ardours of rest and of love,
And the crimson pall of eve may fall
    From the depth of heaven above,
With wings folded I rest on mine airy nest,
    As still as a brooding dove.

What consciousness of power in:

From cape to cape, with a bridge-like shape,
    Over a torrent sea,
Sunbeam-proof, I hang like a roof;
    The mountains its columns be.
The triumphal arch through which I march
    With hurricane, fire, and snow,
When the Powers of the air are chained to my chair,
    Is the million-coloured bow.

Yet the real spirit of the Cloud is playfulness, the
playfulness of a child. Even when the sun has swept
it from the sky, it only laughs:—

I silently laugh at my own cenotaph—
    And out of the caverns of rain,
Like a child from the womb, like a ghost from
        the tomb,
    I arise, and unbuild it again.

It is not only the unlikeness to Byron's gloomy
passion which strikes us in the sublime
childlikeness and bounty and all-embracing love of
this Cloud; there is another characteristic in this
poetry, which we shall merely mention here, and
devote more attention to later, namely, its antique,
its absolutely primitive, spirit. We are reminded of
the most ancient Aryan poetry of nature, of the
Vedas, of Homer. In comparison with this, Byron is
altogether modern. When the Cloud sings:

That orbèd maiden with white fire laden
    Whom mortals call the Moon,
Glides glimmering o'er my fleece-like floor
    By the midnight breezes strewn!

And wherever the beat of her unseen feet
    Which only the angels hear,
May have broken the woof of my tent's thin roof,
    The Stars peep behind her and peer;

and when it speaks of "the sanguine Sunrise, with
his meteor eyes," the poet transports us, by the
primitive freshness of his imagination, back to the
time when the phenomena of nature in all their
newness were transformed into myths.

To Shelley these phenomena were ever new. He
lived among them in a way which no poet had done
before or has done since. By far the greater part of
his short life of thirty years was spent under the
open sky. The sea was his passion; he was
constantly sailing; his most beautiful poems were
written while he lay in his boat with the sun beating
on him, browning his soulful face and delicate
hands. It was a passion that was the pleasure of his
life and the cause of his death. Everything that had
to do with boats and sailing had an attraction for
him. He had a childlike hobby for floating paper
boats; it is said that on one occasion, having no
other paper at hand, he launched a £50 bank-note
on the pond in Kensington Gardens.

He never learned to swim. At the time when he
was constantly, by day and by night, sailing on the
Lake of Geneva with Lord Byron, their boat was
once very nearly upset. Shelley refused all help, and
calmly prepared himself to go down. He afterwards
wrote:

I felt in this near prospect of death, in a
mixture of sensations, among which terror
entered, though but subordinately. My
feelings would have been less painful had I
been alone, but I knew that my companion
would have attempted to save me, and I was
overcome with humiliation when I thought
that his life might have been risked to
preserve mine.

A few years later he had no painful feelings at all in
contemplating such an end. When some months
before his death, Trelawny rescued him from
drowning, all he said was:

It's a great temptation; if old women's tales
are true, in another minute I might have been
in another planet.

In Italy he lived in the open air; now he would be riding with Byron in the country near Venice, Ravenna, or Pisa; now spending whole days in a rowing-boat on the Arno or the Serchio; now out at sea in his yacht. It is interesting to observe how frequently a boat serves him as a simile. He wrote often out at sea, very seldom under the shelter of a roof. *Prometheus* he wrote in Rome, upon the mountainous ruins of the Baths of Caracalla; wandering among the thickets of odoriferous trees on the immense platforms and dizzy arches, he was inspired by the bright blue sky of Rome and the vigorous, almost intoxicating, awakening of spring in that glorious climate. *The Triumph of Life* he wrote partly on the roof of his house at Lerici, partly lying out in a boat during the most overpowering heat and drought. Shelley belonged to the salamander species; broiling sunshine was what suited him best.

It was while lying in a grove on the banks of the Arno, near Florence, that he wrote the most magnificent of his poems, the *Ode to the West Wind*.

In its first stanza the wind is the breath of autumn, driving the dead leaves, "yellow, and black, and pale, and hectic red, pestilence-stricken multitudes"; and of spring, filling "with living hues and odours plain and hill"—we hear it blowing, and we hear its echo in the appealing refrain: "Hear, oh hear!"

In the second stanza we are again reminded of the old mythologies, when the poet sings of the loose clouds on the Wind's stream, "shook from the tangled boughs of heaven and ocean," and of "the locks of the storm" spread on the blue surface of the airy surge "like the bright hair uplifted from the head of some fierce Mænad."

But along with the breath of the West Wind we have Shelley's whole soul in the final outburst:

Oh! lift me as a wave, a leaf, a cloud!
I fall upon the thorns of life! I bleed!

A heavy weight of hours has chained and bowed
One too like thee—tameless, and swift, and proud.

Make me thy lyre, even as the forest is:
What if my leaves are falling like its own?
The tumult of thy mighty harmonies

Will take from both a deep autumnal tone,
Sweet though in sadness. Be thou, Spirit fierce,
My spirit! be thou me, impetuous one!

Drive my dead thoughts over the universe,
Like withered leaves to quicken a new birth;
And, by the incantation of this verse.

Scatter as from an unextinguished hearth
Ashes and sparks, my words among mankind!
Be through my lips to unawakened earth

The trumpet of a prophecy! O Wind,
If Winter comes, can Spring be far behind?"

Compare this Ode with the beautiful passage in the Third Canto of *Childe Harold*, in which Byron cries:

Could I embody and unbosom now
That which is most within me—could I wreak
My thoughts upon expression, and thus throw
Soul, heart, mind, passions, feelings, strong or weak,
All that I would have sought, and all I seek,
Bear, know, feel, and yet breathe—into one word,
And that one word were Lightning, I would speak;
But as it is, I live and die unheard,
With a most voiceless thought, sheathing it as a sword.

Or with his apostrophe to night, during the wild storm on the Lake of Geneva:—

Most glorious night!
Thou wert not sent for slumber! let me be
A sharer in thy fierce and far delight—
A portion of the tempest and of thee!

There could not be a better example of the difference between the attitude towards nature of an all-embracing and an all-defying poetic intellect. Shelley does not, like Byron, desire to possess himself of her thunderbolts. He loves her, not as his weapon, but as his lyre; loves her, unappalled by her gigantic proportions, familiar with her prodigious forces, feeling that the universe is his home. His imagination delights in occupying itself with the heavenly bodies; he is fascinated by their beauty and life as others are by the beauty of the forget-me-not and the rose.

What powerful, all-compelling imagination in the poem which he writes on hearing of the death of Napoleon!

What! alive and so bold, O Earth?
    Art thou not over-bold?
    What! leapest thou forth as of old
In the light of thy morning mirth,
    The last of the flock of the starry fold?
    Ha! leapest thou forth as of old?
Are not the limbs still when the ghost is fled,
And canst thou move, Napoleon being dead?

How! is not thy quick heart cold?
    What spark is alive on thy hearth?
    How! is not *his* death-knell knolled,
And livest *thou* still, Mother Earth?
    Thou wert warming thy fingers old
    O'er the embers covered and cold
Of that most fiery spirit, when it fled—
What, Mother, dost thou laugh now he is dead?

.   .   .   .

'Still alive and still bold,' shouted Earth,
    'I grow bolder and still more bold.
    The dead fill me ten thousandfold
Fuller of speed and splendour and mirth.
    I was cloudy and sullen and cold,
    Like a frozen chaos uprolled,
Till by the spirit of the mighty dead
My heart grew warm: I feed on whom I fed.'

With the eyes of his soul Shelley beheld the soulèd spheres circling in space, glowing within, sparkling without, lighting up the night; his gaze sounded the unfathomable abysses where verdant worlds and comets with glittering hair, and pale, ice-cold moons, glide past each other. He compares them to the drops of dew which fill the flower chalices in the morning; he sees them whirl, world after world, from their genesis to their annihilation, like bubbles on a stream, glittering, bursting, and yet immortal, ever generating new beings, new laws, new gods, bright or sombre—garments wherewith to hide the nakedness of death. He sees them as Raphael painted them in Rome in the church of Santa Maria del Popolo, each governed and guided by its angel; and, wielding the absolute poetic power of his imagination, he assigns to the unfortunate Keats, lately dead, the throne of a yet kingless sphere.

His Witch of Atlas has her home in the ether. Like Arion on the dolphin, she rides on a cloud, "singing through the shoreless air," and "laughs to hear the fire-balls near behind." In this poem Shelley plays with the heavenly bodies like a juggler with his balls; in *Prometheus Unbound* he opens them as the botanist opens a flower. In the Fourth Act of *Prometheus* the earth is represented transparent as crystal; the secrets of its deep heart are laid bare; we see its wells of unfathomed fire, its "water-springs, whence the great sea even as a child is fed," its mines, its buried trophies and ruins and cities. Shelley's genius hovers over its surface, inhaling the fragrant exhalations of the forests, watching the emerald light reflected from the leaves, and listening to the music of the spheres. But to him the earth is not a solid, composite sphere; it is a living spirit, in whose unknown depths there slumbers an unheard voice, the silence of which is broken when Prometheus is unbound.

When Jupiter has fallen, has sunk into the abyss, the Earth and the Moon join in an exulting antiphon, a hymn of praise that has not its equal. The Earth exults over its deliverance from the tyranny of the Deity; the Moon sings its burning, rapturous love-song to the Earth—tells how mute and still it becomes, how full of love, when it is covered by the shadow of the Earth. Its barrenness is at an end:—

    Green stalks burst forth, and bright flowers grow,
    And living shapes upon my bosom move:
        Music is in the sea and air,
        Winged clouds soar here and there,
    Dark with the rain new buds are dreaming of:
            'Tis Love, all Love!

Shelley's imagination resolves nature into its elements, and rejoices over each of them with the naïveté of a child. The Witch of Atlas delights in fire:—

Men scarcely know how beautiful fire is;
    Each flame of it is as a precious stone
Dissolved in ever-moving light, and *this*
    Belongs to each and all who gaze thereon.

And she loves the beauty of sleep:—

A pleasure sweet doubtless it was to see
    Mortals subdued in all the shapes of sleep.
Here lay two sister-twins in infancy;
    There a lone youth who in his dreams did weep;
Within, two lovers linked innocently
    In their loose locks which over both did creep
Like ivy from one stem; and there lay calm
Old age with snow-bright hair and folded palm.

Shelley feels with the streams, which are loved by the sea and disappear in his depths; he sings by the death-bed and bier of nature in autumn and winter; he remembers the flowers that were strewn over Adonis; he describes the goddess of the summer and of beauty, who (like a female Balder) tends the flowers of the gardens; and he paints the progress of the Spirits of the Hours through the heavens (*Arethusa, Hymn of Apollo, Hymn of Pan, Autumn, The Sensitive Plant*, the Hours in *Prometheus Unbound*),

For everything in life and nature he has found the fitting poetic word—for the waste and solitary places,

> Where we taste
> The pleasure of believing what we see
> Is boundless, as we wish our souls to be";

for time,

> Unfathomable sea, whose waves are years!
> Ocean of time, whose waters of deep woe
> Are brackish with the salt of human tears!

for snow, "and all the forms of the radiant frost."

The whole poem in which these last words occur ought to be read. Into it, in a sad mood, he has compressed all his love of nature. It is called simply *Song*, and is addressed to the Spirit of Delight. This Spirit, the poet complains, has deserted him; it forgets all but those who need it not; and such an one as he, can never win it back again, for it is dismayed with sorrow, and reproach it will not hear. Yet, he goes on to say,

> I love all that thou lovest,
> Spirit of Delight!
> The fresh earth in new leaves dressed,
> And the starry night,
> Autumn evening, and the morn
> When the golden mists are born.

> I love snow, and all the forms
> Of the radiant frost;
> I love waves and winds and storms—
> Everything almost
> Which is Nature's, and may be
> Untainted by man's misery.

> I love tranquil solitude.
> And such society
> As is quiet, wise, and good.
> Between thee and me
> What difference? But thou dost possess
> The things I seek, not love them less.

But Shelley's spirit rises on the wings of his sublime enthusiasm for liberty high into the clear air above all these mournful moods. His ode *To a Skylark*, the poem which indicates the transition to the poetry of liberty, is written in a perfect intoxication of joy and freedom from care. It is almost safe to assert that there had been nothing in the older English literature finer in its way than the best of Wordsworth's songs to the lark, which are so typical of the spirit and art of the Lake School.

> Leave to the nightingale her shady wood;
> A privacy of glorious light is thine,

writes Wordsworth; and, as the true conservative poet, he goes on to apostrophise the lark as

> Type of the wise, who soar, but never roam—
> True to the kindred points of Heaven and Home.

Turn from this to Shelley's lark:—

> Like a cloud of fire
> The blue deep thou wingest,
> And singing still dost soar, and soaring ever singest.

We seem to hear all the winds ringing with its "shrill delight," and seem to glide into and be engulfed by a sea of eternally fresh melody. This is the youngest, freshest, gladdest pæan of the pure spirit of freedom. It forms the transition to the long series of poems of freedom, the great group of works in which Shelley's genius is the loud herald of the approaching revolutions. His poetry of freedom is one long war-cry, garbed in ever-changing melodies. Whether it takes the shape of odes to liberty and its champions (poems as beautiful and grand as the Marseillaise), of political satires levelled at customs or persons, of Aristophanic comedy ridiculing the abuses and follies of the day in England, or of mythical or historical tragedy, it is in its essence always the same mighty wail over injustice and hypocrisy, the same powerful appeal to all of his contemporaries who were still capable of feeling anything whatsoever a degradation.

Immediately after his first marriage Shelley began to play the part of a political agitator. He went to Dublin to further the cause of Catholic emancipation, wrote a very juvenile address to the Irish people, in which he besought them to refrain from the violent deeds with which the French Revolution had been stained, and was childish enough to throw down copies of it from the balcony of his hotel, in front of any of the passers-by who looked as if they might be responsive. We gain some idea of the childish spirit in which both he and his young wife regarded the matter, from reading that, one day when they were walking together, he could not resist amusing himself by popping the address into the hood of a lady's cloak, a performance which made his wife, as she herself writes, "almost die of laughing." Shelley attended several political meetings, and on one occasion spoke for more than an hour in the presence of O'Connell and other celebrities. The accounts of his eloquence given by contemporaries are so enthusiastic that they might almost lead us to believe him to have been even greater as an orator than as a poet.

The next time Shelley came into collision with the party in power, the collision was of a much more violent and tragic nature. Harriet was dead, and her father had filed a petition in Chancery to determine which was the fit and proper person to educate her children—he, their grandfather, the retired hotel-keeper, or their father, Shelley, the author of *Queen Mab* and *Alastor*, who was accused of atheism, and would in all probability bring up his children as atheists.

Lord Eldon's judgment was to the effect that, seeing that Shelley's conduct had hitherto been highly immoral, and that, far from being ashamed of this, he was proud of his immoral principles and tried to impress them upon others, the law was in its right in depriving him entirely of the custody of his children, and at the same time decreeing that he should be deprived of a fifth of his income for their maintenance. The children were placed in charge of a clergyman of the Church of England. Shelley felt this blow so terribly that even his most intimate friends never dared speak of the children to him.

In his poem *To the Lord Chancellor* he cries:

I curse thee by a parent's outraged love;
    By hopes long cherished and too lately lost;
By gentle feelings thou could'st never prove;
    By griefs which thy stern nature never crossed.
.   .   .   .

By the false cant which on their innocent lips
    Must hang like poison on an opening bloom;
By the dark creeds which cover with eclipse
    Their pathway from the cradle to the tomb.
.   .   .   .

(By) the despair which bids a father groan,
    And cry, 'My children are no longer mine;
The blood within those veins may be my own,
    But, tyrant, their polluted souls are thine.'

And in the poem to William Shelley, his little son by Mary, he writes:

They have taken thy brother and sister dear,
    They have made them unfit for thee;
They have withered the smile and dried the tear
    Which should have been sacred to me.
To a blighting faith and a cause of crime
They have bound them slaves in youthly time;
And they will curse my name and thee
Because we are fearless and free.
.   .   .   .

Fear not the tyrants will rule for ever,
    Or the priests of the evil faith;
They stand on the brink of that raging river
    Whose waves they have tainted with death.
It is fed from the depths of a thousand dells,
Around them it foams and rages and swells;
And their swords and their sceptres I floating see
Like wrecks, on the surge of eternity.

Fearing that this son of his second marriage might also be taken from him, Shelley left his native country, never to return. At the time when the Lord Chancellor was branding him as less fit for the most rudimentary duties of social life than any other man in England, he was preparing to prove that he was one of the few men then in existence who were predestined to immortality. He left England, stamped as a criminal, and most of the Englishmen whom he met abroad feared and hated him as capable of any crime. He appears to have been actually once or twice subjected to personal molestation.

As already mentioned, Shelley in 1817 published a pamphlet on the subject of Parliamentary Reform. As a proof of the moderation and practicability of the views elaborated in its pages, it need only be mentioned that the Tories in 1867 passed almost the very scheme of Reform which the "atheist and republican" had planned fifty years before. He "disavowed any wish to establish universal suffrage at once, or to do away with monarchy and aristocracy." And on many other occasions he declared himself to be against precipitate changes. His Radicalism consisted simply in his being fifty years ahead of his day.

Attacked and persecuted by the narrow-minded society of the period, Shelley now hurled his poems of liberty at England. His political poems are written with his blood. The employment of such similes for Castlereagh and Sidmouth as "two bloodless wolves whose dry throats rattle" and "two vipers tangled into one," was allowable in his case. It must not be forgotten that to him Castlereagh, Sidmouth, and Eldon, were not men, but personifications of a principle—of the great, fateful principle of reaction to which his career and his happiness had been sacrificed. He writes in *The Masque of Anarchy*:

I met Murder on the way—
He had a mask like Castlereagh.
Very smooth he looked, yet grim;
Seven bloodhounds followed him.

.   .   .   .   .   .

Clothed with the bible as with light,
And the shadows of the night,
Like Sidmouth next, Hypocrisy
On a crocodile came by.

.   .   .   .   .   .

One fled past, a maniac maid,
And her name was Hope, she said,
But she looked more like Despair;
And she cried out in the air:

My father Time is weak and grey
With waiting for a better day;
See how idiot-like he stands,
Fumbling with his palsied hands!

He has had child after child,
And the dust of death is piled
Over every one but me—
Misery! oh Misery!'"

It was not, however, only in bellicose lyrics that Shelley incorporated his political and social ideas and passions at this period. In the year 1818 he wrote two very characteristic narrative poems, *Julian and Maddalo* and *Rosalind and Helen*. The first-mentioned gives a vivid description of the poet's life in Venice with Byron, and affords one of the many proofs of his noble and ardent admiration for Byron's poetry. It contains an account of a visit paid by the two friends to a lunatic asylum in the neighbourhood of Venice and describes the impression produced upon Shelley. The man "whose heart a stranger's tear might wear as water-drops the sandy fountain-stone," and who "could moan for woes which others hear not," could not but be deeply moved by compassion for the unfortunates who at that time were still kept in fetters and punished by flogging.

We gain the best idea of the utter want of understanding of mental disease in those days, and the barbarity displayed in its treatment, from reading of the manner in which an insane patient of such rank as King George the Third was treated in 1798. The King's mental alienation displayed itself chiefly in excessive talkativeness; there was no inclination to any kind of violence. Nevertheless from the very beginning, and throughout the whole duration of the attack, he was kept in a strait-waistcoat, was closely confined, deprived of the use of knife and fork, and subjected to the whims of his pages, who knocked him about, struck him, and used abusive language to him. All this is known because the King retained a distinct remembrance after his recovery of what had happened during his illness.

Shelley's gentleness and love of his fellow-men are evident in the plea which he, ignorant of the humaner treatment of the insane inaugurated in France during the Revolution, utters for these afflicted ones:

Methinks there were
A cure of these with patience and kind care,
If music thus can move.

The second poem, *Rosalind and Helen*, which gives a powerful general impression of the misery which prejudice and intolerance have brought upon the human race, has not hitherto been properly understood or valued according to its deserts. It attempts to give a comprehensive representation of all that truly good and liberal-minded human beings have to suffer from antiquated ideas and principles in combination with human malignity. We have the description of a father who was a coward to the strong, a tyrant to the weak; hard, selfish, false, rapacious; the torturer of his wife and terror of his children, who became pale and silent if they heard, or thought they heard, his footstep on the stair. He dies, and Rosalind, the mother, is distressed because her children involuntarily rejoice at their father's death, and because she herself cannot but feel it to be a relief. The dead man had been strictly orthodox. He has, as it appears when his will is read, decreed that the children shall inherit nothing if they continue to live with their mother, because she secretly holds the Christian creed to be false, and he must save his children from eternal fire. The mother feels that she must leave her children. "Thou know'st," she says—

> Thou know'st what a thing is poverty
>   Among the fallen on evil days.
> 'Tis crime, and fear, and infamy,
>   And houseless want in frozen ways
> Wandering ungarmented, and pain,
> And, worse than all, that inward stain,
> Foul self-contempt, which drowns in sneers
> Youth's starlight smile, and makes its tears
> First hot like gall, then dry for ever.
> And well thou know'st a mother never
> Could doom her children to this ill—
> And well he knew the same.

Rosalind's fate serves, above all else, to show the misery of an unhappy marriage, more particularly the wife's condition of dependence on a bad and tyrannical husband. Shelley's own grief over the loss of his children is also distinctly perceptible in the poem; and Helen's fate recalls the persecution to which the author in his character of philosopher was subjected. The whole representation of Lionel's life and ideas is self-representation. Could there be a better description of Shelley's own love of his fellow-man than this:—

> For love and life in him were twins,
>   Born at one birth. In every other,
> First life, then love, its course begins,
>   Though they be children of one mother."

Young, rich, well-born, Lionel at the time of the Revolution enthusiastically takes his place in the ranks of the reformers whose aim it is to emancipate humanity from the tyranny of creeds.

> Men wondered, and some sneered to see
>   One sow what he could never reap:
> 'For he is rich,' they said, 'and young,
>   And might drink from the depths of luxury.
> If he seeks Fame, Fame never crowned
>   The champion of a trampled creed:
> If he seeks Power, Power is enthroned
>   'Mid ancient rights and wrongs, to feed
> Which hungry wolves with praise and spoil
> Those who would sit near Power must toil.'

The reaction comes:

> None now hoped more. Grey Power was seated
>   Safely on her ancestral throne;
> And Faith, the python, undefeated.
>   Even to its blood-stained steps dragged on
> Her foul and wounded train; and men
> Were trampled and deceived again."

Lionel's enemies succeed in imprisoning him because he has blasphemed their gods. He passes a long time in solitary confinement, separated from the woman he loves. Then he meets her again, and they celebrate their nuptials under the starry sky.

Rosalind and Helen is a poem which bears traces of having been written in a mood of profound despair; in no other work does Shelley go to such extremes in his war upon all traditional law and convention. We have, in a previous volume of this work, touched upon the fact that many writers at the beginning of this century occupied themselves with the theory that the horror of incest has its source in prejudice. Both in *Rosalind and Helen* and in *The Revolt of Islam*, the hero and heroine of which would, but for the earnest entreaties of the publisher, have been brother and sister, Shelley wasted much eloquence on this sinister paradox— which also greatly occupied Byron's mind, and was to give occasion to a foolish and revolting attack upon his memory.

The year 1820 was the year of the scandalous royal divorce case. On the 8th of April 1798, the Prince Regent, compelled by his position to marry, had wedded Princess Caroline of Brunswick. So little regard did he show from the very beginning for even the decencies of the situation, that at their first meeting in St. James's Palace, when the Princess was kneeling before him, he called to Lord

Malmesbury: "Get me a glass of brandy! I don't feel well." Lord Malmesbury asked if a glass of water would not be preferable, upon which the Prince rushed out of the room, swearing, without a word to his fiancée. He was drunk at the wedding, and hiccupped incessantly during the ceremony. Ere long he was not content with displaying the utmost indifference to his wife and slighting her by his liaisons with numbers of other women, but actually treated her with great brutality—kept her in confinement, surrounded her with spies, and, on the ground of a false accusation, took her daughter from her, a proceeding which gave occasion to constant scenes at court. The Princess's conduct does not seem to have been long irreproachable. She was at first only incautious, but in course of time sought consolation in behaviour which was neither blameless nor dignified. At the age of fifty she was travelling all over Europe in the company of her courier and chamberlain Bergami—a man who had formerly been her footman—an Italian Ruy Blas, on whom she conferred one honour and order after another, and whom she loved devotedly.

When, at the time of her husband's accession to the throne, she returned to England, expecting to be crowned Queen, the miserable, contemptible sovereign determined to employ, in procuring a divorce, all the evidence against her which he had obtained by means of paid spies. She was accused before the House of Lords of unfaithfulness. Whole shiploads of foreign hotel waiters and chambermaids were landed in England amidst the angry demonstrations of the populace, to give witness against the Queen. Anything more indecent than this trial it would be difficult to find. Investigations into the positions of bedrooms and beds, descriptions of the clothing or absence of clothing of a Queen and her chamberlain, filled the English newspapers day after day until—the accusation was withdrawn; partly on account of the supposed insufficiency of the proofs, partly on account of the pitch which public contempt for the King, as the author of the scandal, had reached.

It was this divorce case which gave occasion to Shelley's excellent satire, *Œdipus Tyrannus*, or *Swellfoot the Tyrant*, an essay in political comedy. The action of the play passes in Bœotia. A people, who call themselves *Bulls* (*i.e.* John Bulls), nevertheless make their appearance as pigs; consequently, the nature and power and spirit of the English are comprehensively expressed by the word *piggishness*:—

The taxes, that true source of piggishness
(How can I find a more appropriate term
To include religion, morals, peace, and plenty,
And all that fit Bœotia as a nation
To teach the other nations how to live?)
Increase with piggishness itself.

The hypocrisy of the royal husband, the Queen's impudent asseverations of her own chastity, the hypocritical attitude of Castlereagh and Sidmouth—all this is caricatured with the pen of a master.

But Shelley's genius was not of a nature to spend much of its force in satirising the distortions of the age. Untrammelled and ethereal, it was supremely fitted to present to the intellects of the day a glorious conception of the century's ideal of liberty.

And from his boyhood this had been the aim of all Shelley's endeavours. His first works were long, melodious, but, unfortunately, formless poems, which are in their essence protests against kings and priests, against the religions which "people the earth with fiends, hell with men, and heaven with slaves," against the injustice of governments and the servility of the administrators of the law, against compulsory marriages, against the exclusion of women from free competition in bread-winning occupations, against cruelty in the slaughtering of animals. They are protests, in short, against every form of oppression and intolerance, written with no less ambitious an aim than the reformation of humanity, which is to be brought about by showing it how it may remove the causes of its misfortunes and attain to a state which, in comparison with the existing, would be a true golden age.

Shelley had, as he himself laughingly acknowledges, "a passion for reforming the world." In spite of his aversion for didactic poetry, it was (as he puts it in the preface to *The Revolt of Islam*) his object to excite in his reader a generous impulse, an ardent thirst for excellence. He writes:

The panic which, like an epidemic transport, seized upon all classes of men during the excesses consequent upon the French Revolution, is gradually giving place to sanity. It has ceased to be believed that whole generations of mankind ought to consign themselves to a hopeless inheritance of ignorance and misery, because a nation of men who had been dupes and slaves for centuries were incapable of conducting themselves with the wisdom and tranquillity of freemen so soon as some of their fetters were partially loosened … If the Revolution had been in every respect prosperous, then misrule and superstition would lose half their claims to our abhorrence, as fetters which the captive can unlock with the slightest motion of his fingers, and which do not eat with poisonous rust into the soul.

Shelley's purpose was to set forth the principles of the Revolution in a transfigured form. Hence his poetry became a sermon; his imagination embodied, not his observations, but his wishes.

He was firmly persuaded that imagination is the true reformatory power. The man whom crass ignorance has reviled as a materialist had, in the school of Hume and Berkeley, saturated himself with the extremest idealism. To him everything was thought—things were layers of thoughts; the universe itself was but a gigantic coagulation of old thoughts, images, ideas. Hence it is that the poet, whose calling it is to create new imagery of the kind which makes the strongest impression, is always agitating, disturbing, remodelling the world. Says Shelley:

Imagination is the faculty of human nature on which every gradation of its progress—nay, every, the minutest, change—depends.

Either by gently inducing the congealed ideas to flow again, or by forcibly breaking through the crust of outworn opinions, the poet shows himself to be the true reformer.

In his youth devoted to philosophy, but indifferent to history, Shelley, during the one completed period of his life—that preceding the writing of *The Cenci*—sought no foundation in time or space for his visions of reformation; being merely desires, they had no historic reality. And this deficiency entails the absence of various essential qualities in his personages, which only historical and local relations can confer. The qualities they do possess are mainly the deepest seated, original qualities of human nature. In constructing his characters, he goes back to the earliest records of the race. They are half mystical personages— gigantic, vaguely outlined, spiritualised figures; no ordinary human sympathies can lay hold of them, for the reason that "history"—what the ordinary

mind regards as the interesting element in a poem—is despised and ignored by Shelley. Hence his unsuitability for the multitude. An author like Sir Walter Scott will never cease to find a public among all who can read; Shelley will always be the author only of the few elect.

When, however, Shelley chooses a theme suited to his peculiar turn of mind he produces poetry of the very highest rank. His productive gift, from the point of view from which we are now considering it, was of the Greek type; and the same may be said of his religious feeling and of the whole development of his imaginative and reasoning powers. "We are all Greeks," he says somewhere. It was true of himself.

It was, however, only the earliest Greek poetry which treated of such natural phenomena, such gods, and such heroes as we find in Shelley's; therefore it is only with it that his is to be compared. Shelley's lyrics remind us of the Homeric hymns; his political comedy recalls Aristophanes both by its reckless satire and the lyric vigour of its songs, and is worthy of comparison with Aristophanes; it remains to be told that in serious drama he was a worthy rival of Æschylus. His *Prometheus Unbound* is the modern counterpart of the Greek tragedian's *Prometheus Bound*; his *Hellas*, a prophecy of the triumph of Greece, the modern counterpart of *The Persians*.

Let us linger for a moment over *Prometheus*, the magnificent poem in which his poetry of freedom culminates. In Prometheus, Shelley at last found, and succeeded in representing, the typical figure of his poetry and his period. Many types had passed through his mind, amongst others Job and Tasso, who at this time were also engrossing the imagination of Byron and Goethe. He chose Prometheus. High above the lakes and hills of contemporaneous English poetry, Byron's Alps with his Manfred, and Shelley's Caucasus with his Prometheus, soar into the sky.

Ever since the emancipation of the human mind had begun in real earnest, this typical figure had given occupation to all the great poets. It suggests itself about the beginning of our century to Goethe, Byron, and Shelley. Goethe's beautiful poem represents the labours, the artistic productivity, of the human spirit which has freed itself from faith in gods—the man, proud of his hut, which no god built for him, occupied in forming figures in his own image. Goethe's Prometheus is the creative and free. Byron's hard, short, fiery lines describe the martyr who suffers with clenched teeth, silently; from whom no torture can extract confession, and whose ambition it is that no one shall divine his sufferings; this is a Titan who would never, in the manner of the Prometheus of the ancients, have accepted consolation from the daughters of Oceanus or told his woes to them. Byron's is the defiant and bound Prometheus.

Shelley's resembles neither of these. His is the beneficent human spirit which, warring with the principle of evil, is for an immeasurable length of time held in subjugation and tortured by it—and not by it alone, but by all other beings, even the good, who are fooled into accepting evil as necessary and right. He is the spirit who can only for a time be imprisoned and fettered; long as that time may be, the day comes when, to the joy of all, he is released—he is Prometheus unbound, Prometheus triumphant, greeted by the acclamations of all the elements and all the heavenly spheres.

Even during his sufferings he is perfectly calm; for he knows that Jupiter's reign is but a passing period in the life of the universe. He would not exchange his place of torture for all the voluptuous joys of Jupiter's court. When the Furies "laugh into his lidless eyes," and threaten him, he only says:

I weigh not what ye do, but what ye suffer,
  Being evil.

How differently a Byronic Prometheus would have answered! This Titan is full of love—love for his enemies and for the whole human race. Nor have his sufferings closed his heart to the more earthly love passion. In the midst of his agony he remembers his bride—

Asia, who, when my being overflowed,
Wert like a golden chalice to bright wine.

Asia is nature herself, who loves the Titan. She is the child of light, the life of life, whose

            lips enkindle
With their love the breath between them,
And whose smiles, before they dwindle,
    Make the cold air fire.

When the age of suffering and injustice has passed, Jupiter sinks into the abyss of eternity, with cowardly wails and supplications to Prometheus to have mercy on him. The Promethean age begins; the air becomes a sea of sweet, eternally new love melodies; the mighty, deep-toned jubilation of the Earth is heard in alternation with the Moon's enchanting song of bliss; and then the whole universe chimes in in a chorus of rejoicing unsurpassed even by that with which Beethoven's Ninth Symphony ends.

We cannot do much more than allude to the fact that Shelley, after competing with Æschylus, began to produce on Shakespeare's lines. Taking a sudden excursion into the realms of history, he gave England what even Byron pronounced to be the best tragedy written by any of her sons since the days of Shakespeare. *The Cenci* reminds the reader slightly of such a play as *Measure for Measure*, although Shakespeare was not possessed by the ardent hatred of tyranny which inspired Shelley's play.

To the Romans the name of Beatrice Cenci is to this day the great symbol of liberty. The young girl who defended her honour against her atrocious father (whose deed of violence was indirectly sanctioned by the corruption of the rulers of the country from the Pope downwards) is still regarded by the Roman as a heroine and martyr. Whenever, during the long oppression of the Papacy, there has been a little clearing of the air, a little brightening of the horizon, her name has been heard, her picture has circulated, in Rome. Shelley, forgetting all theories, is here entirely absorbed by history. But what evidently impressed him in this tragic collision of duties, was the violent break with all traditional morality which the father's crime necessitated; and he was also attracted by the opportunity the situation offered for throwing a glaring search-light on the accepted theological doctrine of the paternal benevolence displayed in the regulation of the universe. Beatrice says:

        Thou great God,
Whose image upon earth a father is,
Dost thou indeed abandon me?"

And when she is asked:

Art thou not guilty of thy father's death?

She answers:

> Or wilt thou rather tax high-judging God
> That he permitted such an act as that
> Which I have suffered, and which he beheld;
> Made it unutterable, and took from it
> All refuge, all revenge, all consequence,
> But that which thou hast called my father's death?

In the torture chamber she says:

> My pangs are of the mind and of the heart
> And of the soul: ay, of the inmost soul,
> Which weeps within tears as of burning gall
> To see, in this ill world where none are true,
> My kindred false to their deserted selves;
> And with considering all the wretched life
> Which I have lived, and its now wretched end;
> And the small justice shown by Heaven and Earth
> To me or mine; and what a tyrant thou art,
> And what slaves these; and what a world we make,
> The oppressor and the oppressed.

It is plain that what specially attracted Shelley in Beatrice's character was its combination of energy and gentleness.

When the hour of death has come, a horror seizes her at the thought that after death she may meet her father again. She cries:

> If there should be
> No God, no heaven, no earth, in the void world,
> The wide, grey, lampless, deep, unpeopled world!
> If all things then should be my father's spirit,
> His eye, his voice, his touch, surrounding me,
> The atmosphere and breath of my dead life!
> If sometimes, as a shape more like himself,
> Even the form which tortured me on earth,
> Masked in grey hairs and wrinkles, he should come,
> And wind me in his hellish arms, and fix
> His eyes on mine, and drag me down, down, down!
> For was he not alone *omnipotent*
> On earth, and ever present? Even though dead
> Does not his spirit live in all that breathe,
> And work for me and mine still the same ruin,
> Scorn, pain, despair? Who ever yet returned
> To teach the laws of Death's untrodden realm?
> Unjust perhaps as those which drive us now,
> Oh whither, whither?

It was of this, the most mature and best planned of Shelley's works, that the *Literary Gazette* wrote: "*The Cenci* is the most abominable work of the time, and seems to be the production of some fiend." The reviewer hopes never again to see a book "so stamped with pollution, impiousness, and infamy."

The hostility evinced depressed Shelley, who thought that this time he had done his best. He was not intimidated by it, but his desire to produce became less strong. During the last two years of his life no long works came from his pen. In November 1820 he writes:

> The reception the public have given me might
> go far to damp any man's enthusiasm.

His last letters are full of remarks on the criticism meted out to him.

April 1819:—"As to the Reviews, I suppose there is nothing but abuse; and this is not hearty enough or sincere enough to amuse me."

March 1820:—"If any of the Reviews abuse me, cut them out and send them; if they praise, you need not trouble yourself. I feel ashamed if I could believe that I should deserve the latter: the former, I flatter myself, is no more than a just tribute."

In 1821 he writes the poem on Keats with the terrible outburst against the reviewer who is supposed to have been the cause of the young poet's death:

> "Hot shame shall burn upon thy secret brow,
> And like a beaten hound tremble thou shalt—as now."

June 1821:—"I hear that the abuse against me exceeds all bounds. Pray, if you see any one article particularly outrageous, send it me. As yet, I have laughed; but woe to these scoundrels if they should once make me lose my temper. I have discovered that my calumniator in the *Quarterly Review* was the Reverend Mr. Milman. Priests have their privilege."

August 1821:—"I write nothing, and probably shall write no more."

Byron, when his enemies irritated him, stopped his work for a moment and showed them the lion's claw. Shelley was of a different nature. The satire of the reviewers contained in his *Peter Bell the Third* is sportiveness in comparison with Byron's sanguinary attacks on Southey and the others.

Whenever Shelley made his appearance the creeping things of literature began to swarm and stir beneath his feet. They stung his heel; he could not bruise their heads, for such creatures have, as Swinburne has observed, too little head to be perceived and bruised. Byron's poetry had, moreover, made for him friends and admirers by the thousand; he shared Parnassus with Goethe; he had begun to set the stamp of his spirit on the continent of Europe. Shelley was too far in advance of his age. The crowd will follow a leader who marches twenty steps in advance; but if he is a thousand steps in front of them, they do not see and do not follow him, and any literary freebooter who chooses may shoot him with impunity.

Moore was a man of great talent, and exercised influence as such. What Shelley had was not talent, either great or small, but genius. He was the very genius of poetry; and he had all the power which genius gives; where he fell short was in his grip of reality. He has influenced the succeeding generations of English poets throughout this whole century, but he had not the twentieth part of the merely talented Moore's influence upon his own contemporaries. Byron was, as none had ever been before, the poet of personality, and as such was excessively egotistic; prejudice and vanity could not in his case be entirely eradicated without nobler qualities suffering from the process. Shelley, perfectly free from vanity and egotism, was absorbed in his ideals; he expanded his Ego until it embraced the universe. But what was ideal virtue in him as a man entailed a fatal defect in his poetry, at any rate in the works produced during the first part of his too short life. This poet, so devoid of all thought of self, was long entirely deficient in self-restraint. A sense of form as regarded a great composition in its entirety was for many years denied him. In making his first appearance as a poet he stumbled over the threshold, and it takes more than genius to make the reading public forget such an entrance. *The Revolt of Islam*, with all the beauty of its detail, is vague and formless; it hovers transcendentally in the air. With its shadowy, bloodless characters, it is distended to such proportions that it is a task to read it to the end; and it was a task which few accomplished. Until Shelley wrote *The Cenci* he seems to have had no idea of the infinite attractiveness and infinite value of the characteristics of the individual. Even Prometheus

and Asia in their quality of types are destitute of any peculiarly distinguishing feature; their names are merely headings to the most beautiful lyric verse which England has ever produced. *The Cenci* shows how capable Shelley was of acquiring what he was naturally deficient in; but, alas! he was carried off before he could fulfil the rich promise of his youth, and before his contemporaries had had their eyes opened to what they possessed in him. Although his shorter lyrics surpass in depth and freshness, naturalness and charm, everything else in the shape of lyric poetry that the century has produced, they could not influence his own generation, as most of them were not even printed during his lifetime.

Thus Shelley was no more capable than Moore or Landor of bringing about the spiritual revolution of which Europe stood in need and expectancy. It required a poet who was as personal as Shelley was universal, as passionate as Shelley was idealistic, as savagely satirical as Shelley was harmonious and graceful, to perform the Herculean task of clearing the political and religious atmosphere of Europe, awaking the slumberers, and plunging the mighty into the abyss of ridicule. A man was required who could win the sympathies of his age alike by his vices and his virtues, his excellences and his faults. Shelley's instrument was an exquisite violin; a trumpet was what was needed to pierce the air and give the signal for battle.

Little remains to be told of Shelley's life—only the story of his last sail from Leghorn to Lerici, of the sudden gale in which he perished, of the long days spent by his despairing wife in searching the coast, and of the discovery of the almost unrecognisable corpse. The Tuscan law required any object thus cast ashore to be burned. Shelley's body was committed to the flames by Byron and Trelawny with Grecian and pagan observances that were in harmony with his character. Frankincense, wine, salt, and oil, were poured on the fuel. The day was beautiful and the surroundings were glorious—the calm sea in front, the Apennines behind. A curlew wheeled round the pyre, and would not be driven away. The flame arose golden and towering. The body was consumed, but, to the surprise of all, the heart remained entire. Trelawny snatched it from the glowing furnace, severely burning his hand. The ashes were deposited near the Pyramid of Cestius in Rome, which Shelley had spoken of as an ideal resting-place.

The first-mentioned of the men who consigned his body to the flames was his spiritual heir. This man's name is to be read on every page of the history of his day. We see his way prepared by Wordsworth, Coleridge, and Scott; he is hated by Southey, misunderstood by Landor, loved by Moore, admired, influenced, and sung by Shelley. He occupies a place in every one's life. It is he who sets the final and decisive stamp on the poetical literature of the age.

B Y R O N

XVII

BYRON: THE PASSIONATE PERSONALITY

NTERING THE THORVALDSEN MUSEUM IN Copenhagen, and turning to the right, the first work that meets one's eye is the marble bust of a noble-looking young man, with beautiful features and curly hair—the bust of Lord Byron. In room No. 12 we find the same work in plaster, and in No. 13 stands the statue executed (after Byron's death) from the bust. Let us examine the plaster bust, which is without doubt the most speaking likeness. Beauty and distinction are the first qualities that strike us in this head and face; but the next moment we are attracted by an expression of energy, which comes chiefly from a restless quiver of the brow—indicating that clouds might gather on it and lightning flash from the clouds— and from something imperiously compelling in the glance. This brow betokens irresistibility.

When one remembers the dissimilarity of Thorvaldsen's and Byron's natures, remembers that in all probability Thorvaldsen never read a line of Byron's poetry, and also that the poet did not show his best side to the sculptor, the result of the meeting of the two great men must be regarded as extraordinarily satisfactory. The bust gives what is necessarily a feeble and incomplete, but nevertheless a true and beautiful representation of a main aspect of Byron's character which one would hardly have expected Thorvaldsen to grasp. The idyll is that sculptor's real province. When he sets himself to represent Alexander's triumphal entry into Babylon, he is much more successful with the shepherds, the sheep, the fishermen, the women, the children, the procession in general, than with the hero himself; the heroic is not to the same extent his affair; how much less, then, the combatant nature in the complicated, modern form of it which has been dubbed the dæmonic. And yet he understood Byron. In the bust (not in the statue) he has given the world a monument of him, which, although it satisfied neither the Countess Guiccioli nor Thomas Moore, is worthy both of the poet and

of the artist. If Thorvaldsen had really known Byron, the work would probably have been still better; the face would have had a touch of the frankness and attractiveness which impressed all who knew him well. This is absent. But the Danish sculptor has succeeded in penetrating into what lay beneath the gloomy expression which he considered an assumed one, and showing us the suffering, the restlessness, the genius, the noble and terrible power.

It was, undoubtedly, with the Byron of the Museum that the next generation to his in Denmark grew up. But the image presented to them there was invariably connected in their minds with the story of the poet's visit to Thorvaldsen's studio, and with the latter's observation: "It was his fancy to be unhappy;"[7] and they wondered why such a great man should not have been perfectly natural. And so the first attitude of the Danes to Byron was a wrong, or at any rate an uncertain one. And an uncertain one it still remains. He is little fitted to be the hero of the present age. The very things which were much more effectual than his greatness as a poet in arousing the admiration of our grandfathers and grandmothers, are the things that repel the present generation—all those mythical traditions (which really obscure his history to us) of Byron the stage hero, with the tie which every one imitated; Byron, the hero of romance, whose pistols were his constant companions, and whose amorous adventures were as famous as his verse; Byron, the aristocrat, with the title which he valued so highly, but which makes little impression on a generation that recognises no aristocracy but that of the intellect. And our practical age has, moreover, a distinct contempt for what Byron sometimes imagined his honour required him to be, and sometimes really was—the dilettante.

---

[7] Thiele: *Thorvaldsen i Rom.* i. 342.

It was a matter of honour with him to practise his art in a non-professional manner. His position and his pursuits (so he writes in the preface to his first volume of poetry) make it highly improbable that he will ever take up the pen again. In 1814, at the very summit of the celebrity won for him by his first narrative poems, he determines to write no more poetry, and to suppress all that he has written. A month afterwards he writes *Lara*. Jeffrey criticised the character of the hero as too elaborate. Byron asks (in a letter of 1822):

What do they mean by '*elaborate?*' I wrote *Lara* while undressing after coming home from balls and masquerades, in the year of revelry 1814.

We feel that he lays stress on the careless manner of production and the planlessness consequent thereon, from a desire to show that he is not a professional poet, but, in the first instance, a man of the world, in the second, that which his gifts forbade his being, namely, a poetical dilettante.

Though he was incapable of being a dilettante in the calling in which he was determined to play that part (a determination which nowadays detracts from our respect for him), he was indisputably one in another field of activity, where it was by no means his intention, namely, in politics. Practical though he always showed himself to be when it came to political action, his politics were in reality—whether he took part in the conspiracies of the Carbonari at Ravenna or led the Suliotes at Missolonghi—the politics of the emotionalist and the adventurer. His first proceeding after he had resolved to go to Greece was to order for himself and his friends gilded helmets with his crest and motto engraved on them. The great politician of our days is the man who lays plans, adheres to them and develops them year after year, and, obstinate and regardless of side issues, carries them out in the end, without the heroic apparatus, but with the hero's determination.

It must not be forgotten that a whole succession of Byron's admirers and imitators have forced themselves in between him and us, obscuring the figure, and confusing our impression, of the great departed. Their qualities have been imputed to him, and he has been blamed for their faults. When the literary reaction set in against those who had understood him half and wrongly—against the brokenhearted, the *blasés*, the enigmatical,

writers—his great name suffered along with theirs; it was swept aside along with the lesser ones. It had deserved better of fate.

George Gordon Byron, born on the 22nd of January 1788, was the son of a passionate and unhappy mother, who a short time before his birth left her dissipated, brutal husband. This man, Captain Byron, who had served for a time in America as an officer in the Guards, was known in his youth as "mad Jack Byron." He eloped to the Continent with the wife of the Marquis of Carmarthen, married her when her husband obtained a divorce from her, spent all her money, and treated her so badly that she died of grief a few years after her marriage. Captain Byron returned to England with his little daughter, Augusta, and, solely with the view of improving his circumstances, married a wealthy Scottish heiress, Miss Catherine Gordon of Gight, who became the mother of the man who still enjoys a world-wide fame. Immediately after the wedding Captain Byron began to make away with the fortune of his second wife. In the course of a year he had reduced it from £24,000 to £3000. She left him in France and, coming to London, gave birth there to her only child. By an accident, said to have occurred at the time of his birth, one of the child's feet was malformed.

Two years later the mother went with her boy to Scotland, and took up her residence at Aberdeen. Captain Byron, during a pause in his dissipations, followed them there, in the hope of extracting more money from his wife. She generously gave him the shelter of her roof for a time, and afterwards they still continued to visit each other, until Captain Byron, to evade his creditors, was obliged to return to France, where he died in 1791. When the news of his death reached his wife, who had never ceased to love him, her grief bordered on distraction, and her shrieks were so loud as to be heard in the street.

Uncontrollable passionateness, differing only in its manifestations and its force, was thus a characteristic of both Byron's parents. And farther back in the families of both, we find the same temperament, revealing itself in the mother's family in attempts at suicide and poisoning, and in the father's, now in heroic daring, now in reckless excess. Byron's paternal grandfather, Admiral John Byron, generally known as "hardy Byron," took part in the naval warfare against Spain and France, made voyages of discovery in the South Sea, circumnavigated the globe, and went through perils and adventures without number; the peculiarity that he could never take a voyage without encountering terrible storms gained him the nickname among the sailors of "foul-weather Jack." Byron compares his own fate with his grandfather's. The family temperament shows itself in its worst form in the poet's grand-uncle, William, Lord Byron, a dissolute brawler, who achieved notoriety by killing his neighbour, Mr. Chaworth (after a quarrel), in a duel fought without seconds. It was only in his quality of peer of England that he escaped sentence for murder; ever after his trial he lived on his estate of Newstead, shunned like a leper. He was hated by all around him; his wife procured a separation from him; among the superstitious country people extravagantly horrible stories of his doings circulated and were believed.

Thus the poet had wild blood in his veins. But it was also very aristocratic blood. On the mother's side he claimed descent from the Stuarts, from King James the First of Scotland; on his father's he was the descendant (though with a bar-sinister in the arms, a circumstance Byron himself never alludes to) of the Norman noble Ralph de Burun, who accompanied William the Conqueror into England. And when the grand-uncle just named lost, first his only son, and then, in 1794, his only grandson, it became probable that "the little lame boy who lives at Aberdeen," as his uncle called him, would inherit both Newstead and the family title.

It was with this prospect before him that the lame boy grew up. He was proud and uncontrollable by nature. When he was still in petticoats, his nurse reprimanding him angrily one day for having soiled a new frock, he got into one of his "silent rages" (as he himself called them), turned as pale as a sheet, seized his frock with both hands, and tore it from top to bottom. His mother's treatment of him was little calculated to correct these tendencies. She alternately overwhelmed him with reproaches and with passionate caresses; when she was in a rage she vented on him the anger which his father's treatment of her aroused; she sometimes even reproached him with his lameness. The fault lies partly with her that this physical infirmity cast such a dark shadow over little George's mind; he heard his own mother call him "a lame brat." Bandaging and various kinds of surgical treatment only increased the evil; the foot gave him much pain, and the proud little boy exercised all the strength of his will in concealing his suffering, and, as much as possible, his limp. Sometimes he was unable to bear

any allusion to his deformity; at other times he would speak with a mocking bitterness of his "club-foot."

Though Byron was not diligent at school, he developed a passion, the moment he could read, for history and books of travel; the seeds of his longing for the East were sown in his earliest youth. He himself tells that before he was ten he had read six long works on Turkey, besides other books of travel and adventure, and Arabian tales. As a little boy his favourite story was *Zeluco*, by John Moore, the hero of which is a youth whose mother's bad education of him after his father's death has led to his giving way to all his own caprices; he becomes "as inflammable as gunpowder." In this hero of romance, who reminds us of William Lovell, the boy saw himself reflected. One of the qualities which were to play a decisive part in the poet's life revealed itself very early, namely, his passionate attraction towards the other sex. At the age of five he was so deeply in love with a little girl, Mary Duff, that when, eleven years afterwards, he heard of her marriage, his feelings nearly threw him into convulsions.

With pride, passionateness, melancholy, and a fantastic longing for travel, there was combined, as the determining quality of his character, an ardent love of truth. Naïve sincerity distinguished the child who was destined as a man to be the great antagonist of the hypocrisies of European society. His defiant spirit was only one of the forms of his truthfulness. His nurse took him one night to the theatre to see *The Taming of the Shrew*. In the scene between Catherine and Petruchio, where Petruchio insists that what Catherine knows to be the moon is the sun, little Geordie (as they called the child) started from his seat and cried out boldly: "But I say it is the moon, sir."

When George was ten, his grand-uncle, Lord Byron, died. One of the child's first actions after being told what had happened, was to run to his mother and ask if she noticed any difference in him since he had become a lord. On the morning when his name was first called out in school with the title of "Dominus" prefixed to it, he was so much agitated that he was unable to give utterance to the usual answer, "Adsum"; after standing silent for a moment he burst into tears. Byron's intensest pleasures were at first, and for long, those of gratified vanity. But to understand his agitation properly in this case, one must remember what the title of "lord" implied, and still implies, in England.

The nobility proper of that country consists of not more than about four hundred titled persons—about the number of princes in Germany. On their own estates these noblemen exercise an almost unlimited political and social influence; their position is not much inferior to that of reigning princes, and, as a rule, their wealth corresponds to their rank. Such, however, was not the case in this instance; Byron had no private fortune, and the property of Newstead Abbey was in a neglected condition, and heavily mortgaged.

In the autumn of 1798 Mrs. Byron took her little son to Newstead. When they came to Newstead toll-bar, affecting to be ignorant of the neighbourhood, she asked the woman of the toll-house, to whom the park and mansion they saw before them belonged. She was told that the owner of it had been some months dead.

"And who is the next heir?" asked the proud and happy mother.

"They say," answered the woman, "it is a little boy who lives in Aberdeen."

"And this is he, bless him!" exclaimed the nurse, no longer able to contain herself, and turning to kiss with delight the young lord, who was seated on her lap.

In 1801 the boy was sent to Harrow, one of the great English public schools which is much in favour with the aristocracy. The system of instruction (strictly classical) was uninteresting and pedantic, and did not produce much effect on Byron, whose relations with his masters were as strained as his friendships with his comrades were enthusiastic. He writes in his diary in 1821:

My school friendships were with *me passions* (for I was always violent).

As a friend he was generous, and loved to play the part of protector. When Peel, the future Prime Minister, was one day being unmercifully thrashed by the elder boy whose fag he was, Byron interrupted, and, knowing he was not strong enough to fight the tyrant, humbly begged to be allowed to take half the stripes the latter meant to inflict. When little Lord Gort, after having had his hand burned with a piece of red-hot iron by one of the monitors, as a punishment for making bad toast, refused, when the matter was investigated into, to tell the name of the culprit, Byron offered to take him as his fag, promising that he should not be

ill-used. Said Lord Gort (see Countess Guiccioli's *Reminiscences*):

I became his fag, and was perfectly delighted when I found what a good, kind master I had, one who was always giving me cakes and sweets, and was most lenient with my faults.

To his favourite fag, the Duke of Dorset, Byron, in his *Hours of Idleness*, addressed some charming lines in memory of their school days.

When the boy was at home in the holidays, his mother's behaviour towards him was as erratic, her temper as uncontrollable, as ever; but now, instead of being afraid of her, he could not resist laughing at the fat little woman's outbreaks. Not content with smashing cups and plates, she sometimes employed poker and tongs as missiles.[8]

---

[8] The relation between mother and son has been so accurately and vividly described by Disraeli in his novel *Venetia*, that I append a scene from the book in question,—merely condensing it, and substituting the real names for the fictitious (Cadurcis, Plantagenet, Morpeth, &). The scene takes place one morning at Annesley, a country house in the neighbourhood of Newstead. A post-chaise drives up to the hall, and from it issues a short, stout woman with a rubicund countenance, dressed in a style which remarkably blends the shabby with the tawdry. She is accompanied by a boy between eleven and twelve years of age, whose appearance is in strong contrast with his mother's, for he is pale and slender, with long curling black hair and black eyes, which occasionally, by their transient flashes, agreeably relieve a face, the general expression of which might be esteemed somewhat shy and sullen. It is a first visit. The visitors enter tired and hot.

"'A terrible journey,' exclaimed Mrs. Byron, fanning herself as she took her seat, 'and so very hot! George, my love, make your bow! Have not I always told you to make a bow when you enter the room, especially where there are strangers? Make your bow to Mrs. Chaworth.'

The boy gave a sort of sulky nod, but Mrs. Chaworth received it so graciously and expressed herself so kindly to him that his features relaxed a little, though he was quite silent and sat on the edge of his chair, the picture of dogged indifference.

'Charming country, Mrs. Chaworth,' said Mrs. Byron.... 'Annesley is a delightful place, very unlike the Abbey. Dreadfully lonesome, I assure you, I find it there. Great change for us from a little town and all our kind neighbours. Very different from Dulwich; is it not, George?'

'I hate Dulwich,' said the boy.

'Hate Dulwich!' exclaimed Mrs. Byron; 'well, I am sure, that is very ungrateful, with so many kind friends as we always found. Besides, George, have I not always told you that you are to hate nothing? It is very wicked.—The trouble it costs me, Mrs. Chaworth, to educate this dear child!' continued Mrs. Byron turning to her hostess. 'But when he likes, he can be as good as any one. Can't you, George?'

Lord Byron gave a grim smile, seated himself at the very back of the deep chair and swung his feet, which no longer reached the ground, to and fro. 'I am sure that Lord Byron always behaves well,' said Mrs. Chaworth.

'There, George,' continued Mrs. Byron, 'only listen to that. Hear what Mrs. Chaworth says. Now mind, never give her cause to change her opinion.

George curled his lip, and half turned his back on his companions....

'George, my dear, speak. Have not I always told you, when you pay a visit, that you should open your mouth now and then. I don't like chattering children, but I like them to answer when they are spoken to.'

'Nobody has spoken to me,' said Lord Byron in a sullen tone.

'George, my love,' said his mother in a solemn voice, 'you know you promised me to be good.'

'Well! what have I done?'

'Lord Byron,' said Mrs. Chaworth, interfering, 'do you like to look at pictures?'

'Thank you,' replied the little lord in a more courteous tone; 'I like to be left alone.'

'Did you ever know such an odd child!' said Mrs. Byron; 'and yet, I assure you, Mrs. Chaworth, he can behave, when he likes, as pretty as possible.'

'Pretty!' muttered the little lord between his teeth.

'If you had only seen him at Dulwich sometimes at a little tea-party,' said Mrs. Byron, 'he really was quite the ornament of the company.'

'No, I wasn't,' said Lord Byron.

'George!' said his mother again in a solemn tone, 'have I not always told you that you are never to contradict any one?'

The little lord indulged in a suppressed growl.

'There was a little play last Christmas,' continued Mrs. Byron, 'and he acted quite delightfully. Now

Let us imagine, after such a scene as that described in the note, a smiling, golden-haired girl entering the room and softening the defiant boy's mood with a look, and we have a situation such as cannot have been at all uncommon at Annesley, the residence of the Chaworth family (relations of the man whom Byron's grand-uncle killed in the

you would not think that, from the way he sits upon that chair. George, my dear, I do insist upon your behaving yourself. Sit like a man.'

'I am not a man,' said Lord Byron, very quietly; 'I wish I were.'

'George!' said the mother, 'have I not always told you that you are never to answer me? It is not proper for children to answer.... Do you hear me?' she cried, with a face reddening to scarlet, and almost menacing a move from her seat.

'Yes, everybody hears you, Mrs. Byron,' said the little lord.

'Don't call me Mrs. Byron; that is not the way to speak to your mother; I will not be called Mrs. Byron by you.... I have half a mind to get up and give you a good shake, that I have. O Mrs. Chaworth,' sighed Mrs. Byron, while a tear trickled down her cheek, 'if you only knew the life I lead, and what trouble it costs me to educate that child!'

'My dear madam,' said Mrs. Chaworth, 'I am sure that Lord Byron has no other wish but to please you. Indeed you have misunderstood him.'

'Yes! she always misunderstands me,' said Lord Byron in a softer tone, but with pouting lips and suffused eyes.

'Now he is going on,' said his mother, beginning herself to cry dreadfully ... and, irritated by the remembrance of all his naughtiness, she rushed forward to give him what she had threatened, and what she in general ultimately had recourse to, a good shake.

Her agile son, experienced in these storms, escaped in time, and pushed his chair before his infuriated mother; Mrs. Byron, however, rallied, and chased him round the room; in her despair she took up a book and threw it at his head; he laughed a fiendish laugh, as, ducking his head, the book flew on and dashed through a pane of glass. Mrs. Byron made a desperate charge, and her son, a little frightened at her almost maniacal passion, saved himself by suddenly seizing Mrs. Chaworth's work-table and whisking it before her. She fell over the leg of the table, and went into hysterics, while Lord Byron, pale and dogged, stood in a corner."

notorious duel), when Mrs. Byron and her son were visiting there. The golden-haired girl, Mary Anne Chaworth, was seventeen when Byron was fifteen. He loved her passionately and jealously. At balls, where she was in great request as a partner, and his lameness prevented his dancing, it occasioned him agonies to see her in the arms of other men. The climax was put to his sufferings when he overheard her one evening saying to her maid: "Do you think I could care anything for that lame boy?" He darted out of the house, late though it was, and, scarcely knowing where he was running, never stopped till he came to Newstead. Thirteen years later, in the Villa Deodati, by the Lake of Geneva, he wrote, with the tears streaming from his eyes, a poem, *The Dream*, which treats of this attachment, and shows the deep impression made by the early disappointment.[9]

The cleverer Byron became in preserving a sarcastically calm attitude during his mother's fits of rage, the more unnatural became the relations between mother and son. The scenes were sometimes terrible. It is told as a curious example of their idea of each other's violence, that, after parting one evening, each went privately later in the night to the apothecary's to inquire whether the other had been to purchase poison, and to caution the man not to attend to such an application, if made. In his letters young Byron writes with melancholy humour of the manner in which he is every now and then driven to take flight, to escape from scenes at home. He gives not the slightest hint to any one of the intended excursions, for fear, he says, of rousing "the accustomed maternal war whoop."

---

[9] Very characteristic of Mrs. Byron is the manner in which she communicated to her son (two years after he had been obliged to give up all hope) the news of Mary Chaworth's marriage. A visitor who was present tells the story:—"'Byron,' she said, 'I have some news for you.' Well, what is it?' 'Take out your handkerchief first, for you will want it.' He did so, to humour her. 'Miss Chaworth is married.' An expression very peculiar, impossible to describe, passed over his pale face, and he hurried his handkerchief into his pocket, saying, with an affected air of coldness and nonchalance, 'Is that all?' 'Why, I expected you would have been plunged in grief!' He made no reply, and soon began to talk about something else." The less he could confide in his mother, the more impelled he felt to express his feelings and sorrows on paper.

In 1805 Byron went to Cambridge, where he spent his time less in study than in the practice of all the varieties of athletic exercise to which from his childhood he had eagerly devoted himself, in the hope of atoning by his proficiency in them for his bodily infirmity. Riding, swimming, driving, shooting, boxing, cricket-playing, and drinking, were accomplishments in which he was determined to excel. He began to develop the signs of a dandy; and it satisfied his youthful love of bravado to take excursions in company with a pretty young girl, who went about with him in male attire, and played the part of his valet, or sometimes of his younger brother—in which character he was impertinent enough to introduce her to a lady at Brighton who was unacquainted with his family.

Newstead Abbey had been let for a term of years. As soon as it was vacant, Byron went to live there. It is a real old Gothic abbey, with refectory and cells, the earliest parts of it dating from 1170. The house and gardens are surrounded by a battlemented wall. In the courtyard is a Gothic well. In front is a park, with a large lake. At Newstead, Byron and his friends, in their youthful, defiant antipathy to all rules, led a life of dissipation which showed traces of the mania for originality to which, as history shows, men of genius have not unfrequently been subject before becoming conscious of their proper tasks and aims. These young men got up at 2 P.M. and fenced, played shuttlecock, or practised with pistols in the hall; after dinner, to the scandal of the pious inhabitants of the neighbourhood, a human skull filled with Burgundy went round. It was the skull of some old monk, which the gardener had unearthed when digging; Byron, in a capricious mood, had had it mounted in silver as a drinking-cup, and he and his companions took a childish pleasure in using it as such, themselves dressed up as monks, with all the proper apparatus of crosses, beads, tonsures, &.[10] It is a mistake, however, to regard the action simply as an evidence of that want of feeling which so often—among medical students, for instance—accompanies joviality; to a man like Byron the sight of this *memento mori* in the midst of his carousals probably acted as a kind of bitter stimulant. In the lines which he addressed to it he writes that, to the dead man, the touch of human lips must be preferable to the bite of the worm.

---

[10] The present owner of Newstead has, from religious reasons, had it buried.

Byron's excesses did not proceed from too high spirits. He was oppressed, not only by the melancholy which attacks most youths of remarkable ability when they find themselves, with their untried powers, face to face with nothing but questions, but, in addition to this, by the melancholy which was a result of his passionate character and his upbringing. Two stories, which to most of his biographers seem very pathetic, are told of him at this period of his life. The first is in connection with his dog, Boatswain. In 1808, he composed an excessively misanthropic inscription for this favourite's grave, in which he lauds him at the expense of the whole human race; and at the same time he made a will (afterwards cancelled), in which he desired that he should be buried beside his dog, his only friend. The other proof of his forlorn mood is the manner in which he spent his twenty-first birthday, the day of his coming of age, an occasion which is celebrated among the English nobility with all manner of festivities—illuminations, fireworks, a ball, and the entertainment of all the tenants. Byron was so poor that he was obliged to have recourse to the money-lenders for the wherewithal to give his tenants a ball and roast the customary ox for them. But no long train of carriages bringing visitors of high degree drew up at the doors of Newstead Abbey on the 22nd of January 1809; neither mother, sister, guardians, nor relations, near or distant, were there. Byron himself spent the day at a hotel in London. In a letter of the year 1822 he writes:

Did I ever tell you that the day I came of age I dined on eggs and bacon and a bottle of ale? For once in a way they are my favourite dish and drinkable; but as neither of them agree with me, I never use them but on great jubilees—once in four or five years or so.

It is, naturally, pleasanter to be rich than to be poor, and more flattering to one's self-esteem to receive the congratulations of relatives and friends than to feel one's self homeless and solitary; but in comparison with the difficulties and privations and humiliations which every young modern plebeian has to encounter at the outset of his career, the adversities of this young patrician dwindle into nothing. What gave them their importance was that they early drove Byron, who, as a young aristocrat, might otherwise have been absorbed by the pursuits and ideas of his class and kin, exclusively to those resources which he possessed as the single, isolated individual.

It was not one of the great political events of the day, no transport of joy or anger occasioned by the great political revolutions in which the period was so fertile, that tore Byron away from the disorderly, aimless life at Newstead. Such events as the death of Fox, or that proceeding which redounded so little to the honour of England—the bombardment of Copenhagen, made no impression whatever on the youth who, as a man, was to be so strongly affected by every historical occurrence, every political deed or misdeed. It was a private literary contrariety which made the first turning-point in his life. Whilst living (from the summer of 1806 till the summer of 1807) in the little town of Southwell, Byron had produced his first attempts at poetry, which had met with much appreciation from the younger members of a family named Pigot, who were his intimates at the time. In March 1807 a collection of these poems was published under the title, *Hours of Idleness*. The volume contained nothing very remarkable; the poems which really testify to strength of feeling are swamped by quantities of school-boy verses, some of them translations and imitations of the school classics and *Ossian*, the rest, sentimental poems of love and friendship, immature in conception and style. In one or two, we readers of the present day, wise after the event, can plainly detect Byron's future personality and style. In the poem *To a Lady*, which is addressed to Mary Chaworth, occur two genuinely Byronic verses:—

If thou wert mine, had all been hush'd:—
    This cheek now pale from early riot,
With passion's hectic ne'er had flush'd,
    But bloomed in calm domestic quiet.

.   .   .   .   .

But now I seek for other joys:
    To think would drive my soul to madness;
In thoughtless throngs and empty noise,
    I conquer half my bosom's sadness.

The poems were really of little value, and the ample provision of childish, foolish notes, the pretentious preface, and the appendage of the words "A Minor" to the author's name on the title-page, lent themselves to ridicule.

In January 1808, the *Edinburgh Review*, at that time the highest literary court of appeal, contained an extremely sarcastic review of the volume, probably written by Lord Brougham. The reviewer writes:

The noble author is peculiarly forward in pleading minority; we have it in the title-page, and on the very back of the volume … If any suit could be brought against Lord Byron, for the purpose of compelling him to put into court a certain quantity of poetry, and if judgment were given against him, it is highly probable that an exception would be taken, were he to deliver *for poetry* the contents of this volume. To this he might plead *minority*; but, &c. &c … Perhaps however, in reality all that he tells us about his youth is rather with a view to increase our wonder than to soften our censures. He possibly means to say, 'See how a minor can write! This poem was actually composed by a young man of eighteen, and this by one of only sixteen!' … So far from hearing, with any degree of surprise, that very poor verses were written by a youth from his leaving school to his leaving college, inclusive, we really believe that it happens in the life of nine men in ten who are educated in England, and that the tenth man writes better verse than Lord Byron … We must beg leave seriously to assure him that the mere rhyming of the final syllable, even when accompanied by the presence of a certain number of feet—nay, although (which does not always happen) those feet should scan regularly, and have been all counted accurately upon the fingers—is not the whole art of poetry. A certain portion of liveliness, somewhat of fancy, is necessary to constitute a poem … &c. &c.

The reviewer's advice to Byron is to give up poetry and employ his gifts and his leisure hours better. As an exhortation addressed to the epoch-making English poet of the age by one whose profession it was to assay and value the works of literary aspirants, the article, in spite of its partial justification, was undeniably a gross blunder. But as far as Byron himself was concerned, nothing better could have happened to him. It affected him like a challenge; it was a terrible blow to his vanity, and roused that which was to survive him—his pride. A friend who saw him in the first moments of excitement after reading the article, has described the fierce defiance of his looks, and added that it would be difficult for sculptor or painter to imagine a subject of more fearful beauty than the young poet in his wrath.

Byron concealed his feelings from every one. In a letter written about this time he expresses regret that his mother has taken the affair so much to heart, and assures his correspondent that his own repose and appetite have not been discomposed—that these "paper bullets of the brain" have only taught him to stand fire. But a dozen years afterwards he writes:

I well recollect the effect which the critique of the Edinburgh Reviewers on my first poem had upon me—it was rage and resistance, and redress; but not despondency nor despair. A savage review is hemlock to a sucking author, and the one on me knocked me down—but I got up again … bent on falsifying their raven predictions, and determined to show them, croak as they would, that it was not the last time they should hear from me.

Thus came the stimulus from the outside world which for the first time drove all the young man's passionate, scattered emotions into one channel, and made of them one feeling, one aim. With obstinate determination he set to work; he slept during the day, rising after sunset in order to be less disturbed, and for several months worked every night and all night long at his first famous satire.

XVIII

BYRON: THE PASSIONATE PERSONALITY—(*Continued*)

F AMOUS IT IS, AND FAMOUS IT DESERVED to become, though not because of its wit and humour, for it has neither the one nor the other—nor yet because of its effectiveness, for it is satire which for the most part hacks and hews blindly, here, there, and everywhere—but because of the power, the self-consciousness, the unexampled audacity, which underlie and which found expression in the whole. The attacks of the reviewers had produced in Byron for the first time the feeling which was soon to become constant and dominant in his breast, the feeling which first made him completely conscious of himself, and which may be expressed in the words: "Alone against you all!" To him, as to the other great combative characters of history, this feeling was the elixir of life. "Jeer at *me* with impunity! Crush *me*, who am stronger than all of them together!" was the refrain that rang in his ears whilst he wrote. The Edinburgh Reviewers were accustomed, when they crushed a trumpery little poet and flung him on the ground like a fly, or by mischance shot a poor little song-bird, to no resistance on the part of the victim. He either rebelled against the verdict in silence, or humbly laid the blame on his own want of ability. In either case what followed was profound silence. But now they had lighted upon the man whose prodigious strength and weakness lay exactly in the peculiarity that he never blamed himself for a misfortune, but furiously turned upon others as its authors. In this case, too, a silence of a year and a half followed upon the review. But then happened what we read of in Victor Hugo's poem (*Les Châtiments.* "La Caravane"):

Tout à coup, au milieu de ce silence morne
Qui monte et qui s'accroît de moment en
　　moment,
S'élève un formidable et long rugissement!
C'est le lion.

And the image is the correct one. For this satire, with its deficiency in beauty, grace, and wit, is more a roar than a song. The poet who has the throat of the nightingale, rejoices when he for the first time hears that his own voice is melodious; the ugly duckling becomes happily conscious of its swan-nature when it is cast into its own element; but the roar which tells him that now he is grown up, that now he is a lion, startles the young lion himself. It is in vain, therefore, to look in *English Bards and Scotch Reviewers* for sword-thrusts, given with a steady hand and sure aim; these wounds are not the work of a hand; they are torn with a claw—but the claw is the claw of a lion. It is in vain to search for criticism, moderation, reason; does the wounded beast of prey display discernment and tact when a bullet, intended to kill it, has only slightly wounded it? No; its own blood, which it sees flowing, dims its eyes, and it desires nothing but to shed blood in revenge. It does not even seek the firer of the shot alone; if one of the troop has wounded the young lion, then woe to the troop! All the literary celebrities of England, even the greatest and most popular—all who were in favour with the *Edinburgh Review* and all who wrote in it—are in this satire treated like schoolboys by a youth of twenty, scarcely more than a schoolboy himself. They run the gauntlet one after the other, English poets and Scotch reviewers. There is many a hard hit that does not miss its mark. The empty fantasticalness of Southey's *Thalaba*, and its author's abnormal productivity; the proofs afforded by Wordsworth's own poems of the truth of his doctrine that verse is the same as prose; Coleridge's childish naïveté; Moore's licentiousness—all these receive their due share of attention. An attack is made on Scott's *Marmion* which reminds us of the jeers of Aristophanes at the heroes of Euripides. But by far the greater proportion of the attacks made, are so rash and graceless that they became the occasion of much more annoyance to their author

45

than to the persons attacked. Byron's guardian, Lord Carlisle, to whom he had but lately dedicated *Hours of Idleness*, but who had declined to introduce him to the House of Lords; and men like Scott, Moore, and Lord Holland, who at a later period were among the poet's best friends, were here abused on perfectly incorrect premises, and with a want of judgment which is paralleled only by the astonishing alacrity with which Byron, as soon as he was convinced that he had been in the wrong, apologised and strove to efface the impression of his errors. Some years later he tried in vain to put an end to the existence of the satire by destroying the whole fifth edition.

In the meantime it created a great sensation, and produced the desired effect, the rehabilitation of its author.

In the beginning of 1809 Byron had gone to live in London, partly to superintend the publication of his satire, partly for the purpose of taking his seat in the House of Lords. As he had no friend among the peers to introduce him, he was obliged, contrary to custom, to present himself alone. His friend, Mr. Dallas, has described the scene. When Byron entered the House he was even paler than usual, and his countenance betrayed mortification and indignation. The Chancellor, Lord Eldon, put out his hand warmly to welcome him, and paid him some compliment. But this was thrown away upon Lord Byron, who made a stiff bow, and put the tips of his fingers into the Chancellor's hands. The Chancellor did not press a welcome so received, but resumed his seat. Byron carelessly seated himself on one of the empty Opposition benches, remained there for a few minutes to indicate to which party he belonged, and then left. "I have taken my seat," he said to Dallas, "and now I will go abroad."

He left England in June 1809. He had, as he wrote to his mother in 1808, long felt, that

> if we see no nation but our own, we do not give mankind a fair chance—it is from *experience*, not books, we ought to judge of them. There is nothing like inspection, and trusting to our own senses.

He now went first to Lisbon (see the poem *Huzza! Hodgson!*) The description of Cintra in the First Canto of *Childe Harold* is a recollection of the impressions received during his short stay in Portugal. From Lisbon he and his friend Hobhouse travelled on horseback to Seville and Cadiz, and thence to Gibraltar by sea.

None of the magnificent historical monuments of Seville made any impression on Byron, but both there and at Cadiz he was deeply interested in the women. The advances made by various beautiful Spanish ladies flattered the young man, who took with him as a remembrance from Seville a lock of hair about three feet in length. Gibraltar, being an English town, is, of course, a "cursed place."

But, though little impressed by the historical memories of the countries he is visiting, he is already beginning to interest himself in their political relations. Those of Spain with England occupy him first. The first two cantos of *Childe Harold* show that he felt nothing but contempt for the foreign policy of England. He jeers at what the English called their victory of Talavera, where they lost 5000 men without doing the French much harm; and he is audacious enough to call Napoleon his hero.

From Spain Byron went to Malta. Its memories of the days of yore, which so delighted old Sir Walter Scott, made no more impression on the young nobleman than those of Seville had done. He was as entirely devoid of the romantic historical sense as of romantic national feeling. What he thought of, and longed for, were not the green pastures of England, or the misty hills of Scotland, but the Lake of Geneva in all its glory of colour, and the bright Ægean Sea. His mind did not dwell on the historical exploits of his countrymen, on wars like the War of the Roses; it was occupied with the politics of the day; and in the past nothing interested him but the great struggles for liberty. To him the old statues were only stone; the living women were more beautiful in his eyes than the ancient goddesses ("than all the nonsense of their stone ideal," as he puts it in *Don Juan*); but on the field of Marathon he fell into a deep reverie, and he celebrates its memories in both his long narrative poems. When, during the last year of his life, he visited Ithaca, he rejected all offers to show him the remains of antiquity on the island, remarking to Trelawny:

> I detest antiquarian twaddle. Do people think I have no lucid intervals, that I came to Greece to scribble more nonsense?

The poetic enthusiasm for liberty was in the end swallowed up by the practical. With Byron Romantic sentimentality comes to an end; with him the modern spirit in poetry originates; therefore it was that he influenced not only his own country but Europe.

At Malta he was greatly captivated by a beautiful young lady, a Mrs. Spencer Smith, who for political reasons was subjected to persecution by Napoleon. An enthusiastic friendship sprang up between the two, which is commemorated in several of Byron's poems. (*Childe Harold*, ii. 30. *To Florence. Lines Written in an Album, Stanzas composed during a Thunderstorm. Stanzas Written in Passing the Ambracian Gulf.*) From Malta the travellers went by way of Western Greece to Albania, the "rugged nurse of savage men," as Byron in *Childe Harold* calls the country,

(Where) roams the wolf, the eagle whets his beak,
Birds, beasts of prey, and wilder men appear.

It is characteristic of him, that in his first travels he visited regions which lay practically without the pale of civilisation, countries where the personality of the inhabitant was almost entirely untrammelled by convention. Natural affinity attracted him to these scenes and these beings. Like the young man in Wordsworth's *Ruth*,

Whatever in those climes he found
Irregular in sight or sound
Did to his mind impart
A kindred impulse, seem'd allied
To his own powers, and justified
The workings of his heart.

A direct descendant of Rousseau, he had a strong sympathy for all the races still living in "the state of nature."[11] The Albanians were at that time almost as savage as their Pelasgian ancestors. Their law was the law of the sword, the vendetta their idea of justice. The people of the country, as Byron first beheld them assembled, the setting sun illuminating their magnificent dresses and the rich trappings of their horses, whilst drums beat and the muezzins called the hour from the minaret of the mosque, presented such a spectacle as we read of in the *Thousand and One Nights*.

Janina proved to be a more important town than Athens. It was on their journey to or from Janina that the travellers were deserted by their guide. In their perilous condition among these wild mountains, with the prospect before them of dying of hunger, Byron was the member of the party who kept up the spirits of all the others by that dauntlessness which distinguished him in all dangerous situations.

The day after their arrival in the capital, Byron was introduced to Ali Pacha, "the Turkish Bonaparte," whom he had always admired in spite of his savage cruelty. Ali received his visitor standing, was extremely friendly, desired his respects to Byron's mother, and flattered Byron himself very agreeably by telling him that he knew him at once to be a man of noble birth by his small ears, curling hair, and little white hands. The visit to Ali provided matter for some of the principal scenes in the *Fourth Canto* of Don Juan. Lambro and several other Byronic figures are drawn from him. (He is also described by Victor Hugo in *Les Orientales*.) Ali treated Byron like a spoiled child, sending him almonds and sugared sherbet, fruit and sweetmeats, twenty times a day.

Protected by a guard of fifty men given him by Ali from the numerous troops of brigands which infested the country, Byron now travelled all through Albania. His wild followers became so attached to him that, when he had an attack of fever, they threatened to kill the doctor if the patient were not cured. The doctor ran away— and the patient recovered. It was in the course of this tour, before retiring to rest for the night in a cave by the shore of the Gulf of Arta, that Byron saw the scene (the Pyrrhic war-dance to the accompaniment of song) which he afterwards described in *Childe Harold*, ii. 71, 72, and which inspired the beautiful song, "Tambourgi, Tambourgi!"

During his stay in Athens, the indignation he felt at the plundering of the Parthenon by England, in the person of Lord Elgin, inspired him with the poem, *The Curse of Minerva*; and a transient attachment to one of the daughters of the English

---

[11] Byron has described Rousseau in a stanza which might have been written about himself:—
Here the self-torturing sophist, wild Rousseau,
The apostle of affliction, he who threw
Enchantment over passion, and from woe
Wrung overwhelming eloquence, first drew
The breath which made him wretched; yet he knew
How to make madness beautiful, and cast
O'er erring deeds and thoughts a heavenly hue
Of words, like sunbeams, dazzling as they pass'd
The eyes which o'er them shed tears feelingly and fast.
Childe Harold, iii 77.

consul produced the song, *Maid of Athens*, the heroine of which, even after she had become a little pale old lady, continued to be tormented with visits from English tourists. On the 3rd of May, Byron performed his famous feat of swimming across the Dardanelles, from Sestos to Abydos, in an hour and ten minutes; he writes of it in *Don Juan*, and was proud of it all his life.

All that he saw and did on this tour was, a few years later, to provide him with poetic material. In Constantinople he one day saw the street dogs devouring the flesh of a corpse; on this real scene are based the descriptions of horrors in *The Siege of Corinth* and in the Eighth Canto of *Don Juan* (assault of Ismail). After his return to Athens from a tour in the Morea, he would seem himself to have been concerned in the love affair on which *The Giaour* is based. (See the Marquis of Sligo's letter to Byron.) What we know for certain is, that one day, as he was returning from bathing at the Piraeus, he met a detachment of Turkish soldiers carrying, sewn up in a sack, a young girl, who was to be thrown into the sea because she had accepted a Christian as her lover. Pistol in hand, Byron compelled the savage troop to turn back, and partly by bribery, partly by threats, procured the girl's release.

This life of travel and adventure did not produce the mental equilibrium which Byron lacked. His last letters from abroad reveal settled melancholy. The disgust with life which is the result of aimlessness seems to weigh him to the earth. And he feels that he is coming home deep in debt, "with a body shaken by one or two smart fevers," and to a country where he has no friends. He expects to be met only by creditors. What did meet him was the news of his mother's dangerous illness. He hastened to Newstead to see her once more, but she had died the day before he arrived. Her maid found him in the evening sitting beside the corpse. She had heard his sobs through the closed door. On her begging him to try to control his grief, he burst into tears, and exclaimed:

Oh, Mrs. By, I had but one friend in the world, and she is gone!"

Nevertheless, his excessive dislike to his grief being witnessed by others, was sufficient to prevent his following his mother's remains to the grave.

He stood at the Abbey door till the funeral procession had moved off; then, turning to his attendant, young Rushton, desired him to fetch the sparring-gloves, and proceeded to his usual exercise with the boy. At last, the struggle to keep up seeming too much for him, he flung away the gloves and retired to his room. During the protracted fit of melancholy into which he sank, he made a will, in which he again ordered that he should be buried beside his dog.

Byron had hardly landed before his friend Dallas asked him if he had brought any poetry back with him from his travels. The young poet, who was tolerably destitute of the critical sense, produced, not without pride, *Hints from Horace*, a new satire in Pope's style. With this work Mr. Dallas was very justifiably disappointed. On returning it next morning he asked if his friend had written nothing else, on which Byron handed him some short poems, and what he called "a number of stanzas in Spenser's measure" chiefly descriptive of the countries he had visited. These last were the first two cantos of *Childe Harold*; and at the urgent request of Dallas they were at once given to the printer.

In the mind of the reader of today, the impression produced by these two cantos is apt to be mixed up with that produced by the last two (written six or seven years later); but whoever desires to understand Byron's development must be careful to keep the two impressions perfectly distinct from each other. The gap between the first and the second half of *Childe Harold* is as wide as the gap between this same second half and *Don Juan*.

The stanzas which Byron showed Dallas are melodious, sincere in feeling, and occasionally grand; they were the first of the full, harmonious strains which were henceforward to issue from the lips of this poet as long as he breathed the breath of life. But they only faintly forecast what the man was to be, with whose fame, ten years later, the continent of Europe rang. As yet, powerful descriptions of nature form the main ingredient in his poetry; the lyric outbursts are few and far between; to the casual reader these stanzas would seem simply to convey a world-weary young English aristocrat's impressions of travel, ennobled by the stateliness of the style—for the tone of *Childe Harold* is as idealistic and serious as that of *Don Juan* is realistic and humorous.

The mood is one of monotonous melancholy. Byron is not yet the poet who bounds from one feeling to another, by preference its exact opposite, in order to make each as strong as possible, and then hacks and hews at them—the harder, the extremer the tension he has produced. But though we as yet only catch the outline of this poet's countenance, though we perceive nothing of its keenly satirical expression or of its now impudent, now merry smile, we nevertheless divine from the fervent youthful pathos that we are in the presence of the strongest personality in the literature of the day. There is an Ego in this poem which dominates every detail, an Ego which does not lose itself in any feeling, does not forget itself in any cause.

The other literary personalities of the day could metamorphose—could etherealise, liquefy, crystallise—themselves; they could become invisible behind another personality, or transform themselves into cosmic beings, or merge themselves entirely in sensations received from without; but here we have an Ego which, whatever happens, is always conscious of itself, and always comes back to itself; and it is an agitated, passionate Ego, of whose emotions the movement of even the most unimportant lines reminds us, as the whisper of the shell reminds us of the roar of the ocean.

Childe Harold (in the first draft Childe Burun) leaves his country after an ill-spent youth, in a mood of splenetic melancholy, leaving behind no friends and no loved one. His is the youthful weariness of life induced by a constitution and state of health inclining to melancholy, and by an all too early satiety of pleasure. There is not a trace in him of the confident gaiety of youth or of its desire for amusement and fame; he believes, little as he has seen of life, that he has done with everything; and the poet is so completely one with his hero that not for one moment does he ever soar above him on the wings of irony.

All this, which made such a powerful impression on the public of Byron's day, is tolerably unattractive to a critical modern reader; the aim at effect is plainly discernible, and the time when vague world-weariness was interesting is past. But no one with a practised eye can fail to see that in this case the mask—for mask it is—covers an earnest and a suffering countenance. The mask is that of a hermit; pluck it off, and there still remains a man of a solitary nature! The mask is grandiose melancholy; throw it away; beneath it there is real

sadness! Harold's shell-bedecked pilgrim's cloak may be nothing but a kind of ball domino; but it covers a youth of ardent feelings, with a keen understanding, gloomy impressions of life, and an unusually strong love of freedom. In Childe Harold's better Ego there is no insincerity; Byron himself will be answerable for all his hero thinks and feels. And to those who remember what Byron's own conduct, immediately after he wrote *Childe Harold*, was, and who see a direct contradiction between the fictitious personage's elderly melancholy and the real personage's youthfully ardent pursuit of sensual pleasures, we reply, that the reason of the apparent contradiction is simply this—that Byron, who in his poetry was still an idealist, was unable to reveal his *whole* nature in the earlier cantos of *Childe Harold*. All that is there is certainly Byron, but there was in him, along with this, another and perfectly different man; and it was not until he wrote *Don Juan* that he succeeded in introducing this other Byron, as he lived and thought and spoke, into his poetry. The incompleteness of the self-description must not be mistaken for simulation or affectation.

In February 1812 Byron made his maiden speech in Parliament. He spoke in behalf of the poor weavers of Nottingham, whom it was proposed to punish most severely for having destroyed the machinery that was depriving them of their bread. It is a youthful and rather elaborate speech, but full of life and warmth. Byron was quite in his element in pleading the cause of the starving and desperate crowd. He very sensibly pointed out to his countrymen that a tenth part of the sum which they had willingly voted to enable the Portuguese to carry on war, would be sufficient to relieve the misery which it was proposed to reduce to silence by imprisonment and the gallows. Byron's vigorous and obstinate hatred of war is one of the grains of sound commonsense which are to be found in solution in his poetry; it lends animation to the earlier cantos of *Childe Harold*.

His second Parliamentary speech was on the subject of Catholic Emancipation. Though it did not please, it is an excellent one; in it Byron acknowledges, and with correct logic disposes of, one of the arguments against giving religious liberty to the Catholics, namely, that it might equally well be given to the Jews. In reference to this same emancipation question, we find the following youthfully facetious entry in his notebook:

On one of the debates on the Catholic question, when we were either equal or within one (I forget which), I had been sent for in great haste to a ball, which I quitted, I confess, somewhat reluctantly, to emancipate five millions of people.

Playful utterances of this kind (as another example of which take his saying:

After all we must end in marriage; and I can conceive nothing more delightful than such a state in the country, reading the county newspaper, &c., and kissing one's wife's maid")

have, because they are so little in keeping with Childe Harold's melancholy, amply proved to stupid people that nothing was sacred to him. The truth was that, being very young and somewhat of a coxcomb, he considered it derogatory to his dignity to express himself with any feeling; he unconsciously adopted as his motto the saying of St. Bernard: *Plus labora celare virtutes quam vitia!*

The maiden speech was a great success, and helped to draw the attention of the public to the first two cantos of *Childe Harold*, which came out only two days after the speech had been made. The impression produced by *Childe Harold* was astounding; Byron instantaneously became a celebrity—London's new lion, the lawful sovereign of society for the year 1812. The metropolis, as represented by its most beautiful, most distinguished, most brilliant, and most cultivated inhabitants, prostrated itself at the feet of this youth of twenty-three. If these earlier cantos of *Childe Harold* had been distinguished by the qualities of the later, namely, profound originality and vigorous honesty, they would not have made the noise in the world they did. Great honesty and great originality never find favour at once with the general public. It was the veiledness, the vague weariness of the world and its pleasures, which impressed the crowd; the power of which they caught a glimpse, produced all the more effect by revealing itself in a somewhat theatrical manner.

This was the heyday of dandyism. The upper class of London society, with Beau Brummell as its master of ceremonies, gave itself up to a luxuriousness and licentiousness which had not had their parallel since the days of Charles II.

Dinner-parties and balls, the play-house, the gaming-table, pecuniary entanglements, amorous intrigues, seductions and the duels consequent thereon, occupied the days and nights of the aristocracy. And Byron was the hero of the day— nay, of the year. Could there have been a more suitable object for the admiration and worship of a society which was bored and burdened by its own inanity? So young, so handsome, and so wicked! For no one doubted but that he was as dangerous a roué as his hero. Byron had not Scott's coldbloodedness and mental equilibrium to oppose to temptations and flattery. He allowed himself to glide with the stream which supported him on its surface. The artist in him craved for an experience of every mood, and rejected none. He maintained his fame as a poet with ease; there followed on one another with short intervals his narrative poems, *The Giaour* (May 1813), *The Bride of Abydos* (December of the same year), and *The Corsair* (completed on New Year's Day 1814). Of this last work 13,000 copies were sold in one day. The bitter *Ode to Napoleon*, on the occasion of his abdication, showed that Byron, in his pursuit of poetry, was not entirely oblivious of the political events of the day. In 1815 he wrote *Parisina* and *The Siege of Corinth*. The novelty, the foreignness, and the passion of these works, entranced the blasé aristocratic society of London. Their author was the prodigy on whom all eyes were turned. In the drawing-rooms young ladies trembled with the delightful hope that he might take them in to dinner, and at the dinner-table hardly dared to partake of what was set before them, because it was known that he did not like to see women eating. Owners of albums in which he had deigned to write a few lines were objects of envy. A specimen of his handwriting was in itself a treasure. People talked of all the Greek and Turkish women to whom his love must have meant death, and wondered how many husbands he had killed. His brow and his glancing eye suggested wickedness. He wore his hair unpowdered, and it was as wild as his passions. Different in everything from ordinary mortals, he was as abstemious as his Corsair; the other day at Lord -----'s had he not let eleven courses go by untasted and asked for biscuits and soda-water? What an uncomfortable position for the lady of the house, who was so proud of her cook! And what an extraordinary piece of eccentricity in a country where a hearty appetite is one of the national virtues!

We see Childe Harold transformed into Don Juan. The solitary pilgrim becomes the drawing-room lion. On the ladies, Byron's rank, youth, and remarkable beauty naturally made almost more impression than his poetry. In the Life of Sir Walter Scott we find the following opinion given by him on the subject of his fellow-author's personal appearance:

As for poets, I have seen, I believe, all the best of our own time and country—and, though Burns had the most glorious eyes imaginable, I never thought any of them would come up to an artist's notion of the character except Byron … And the prints give one no impression of him—the lustre is there, but it is not lighted up. Byron's countenance is a thing to dream of.

One of the beauties of the day said to herself the first time she saw him: "That pale face is my fate."

Women had, undoubtedly, always occupied a large share of Byron's time and thoughts; but expressions in Childe Harold gave rise to the report that he had maintained a regular harem at Newstead—the harem appearing as a matter of fact to have consisted of one odalisque. Absurdly exaggerated stories were in circulation of the amorous adventures in which he had played the part of hero during his travels. The consequence of all this was that he was positively besieged by women; his table was covered every day with letters from ladies, known and unknown to him. One came to his house (probably in imitation of Kaled in Lara) disguised as a page; many came undisguised. He told Medwin that one day very soon after his wedding he found three married ladies in his wife's drawing-room, whom he at once recognised as "all birds of the same feather."

This life, crowded with empty pleasures and with triumphs for his vanity, at any rate suited Byron better than quiet; for, as he says in Childe Harold, "quiet to quick bosoms is a hell." But, in all this whirl of excitement, did his heart ever really come into play? It would seem not. The love-affair which engrossed him much at this time and also influenced his future, was, as we know from his own letters, only a whirlpool within the whirlpool, and as such attracted him; but it left his heart quite cold.

Lady Caroline Lamb, a young lady of good family, and wife of the statesman afterwards known as Lord Melbourne, had long cherished an ardent desire to make the acquaintance of the author of Childe Harold. Hers was a wild, fantastic, restless nature, which rebelled against every kind of control and promptly followed the inspiration of the moment; therefore she was in so far a kindred spirit of the poet. She was three years older than Byron, fair-haired, with a slender, beautiful figure, and a soft voice; her manner, though affected, was exceedingly attractive. She played in Byron's life the part which Frau von Kalb played in Schiller's.[12] Her connection with him made the lady so much talked of, that her mother did

---

[12] In Lady Morgan's Memoirs we find the following lively account by Lady Caroline Lamb herself of the beginning of her acquaintance with Byron:—"Lady Westmoreland knew him in Italy. She took on her to present him. The women suffocated him. I heard nothing of him, till one day Rogers (for he, Moore, and Spencer, were all my lovers)—Rogers said, 'You should know the new poet,' and he offered me the MS. of Childe Harold to read. I read it, and that was enough. Rogers said, 'He has a club-foot, and bites his nails.' I said, 'If he was as ugly as Æsop I must know him.' I was one night at Lady Westmoreland's; the women were all throwing their heads at him. Lady Westmoreland led me up to him. I looked earnestly at him, and turned on my heel. My opinion in my journal was, 'mad—bad—and dangerous to know.' A day or two passed; I was sitting with Lord and Lady Holland, when he was announced. Lady Holland said, 'I must present Lord Byron to you.' Lord Byron said, 'That offer was made to you before; may I ask why you rejected it?' He begged permission to come and see me. He did so the next day. Rogers and Moore were standing by me: I was on the sofa. I had just come in from riding. I was filthy and heated. When Lord Byron was announced, I flew out of the room to wash myself. When I returned, Rogers said, 'Lord Byron, you are a happy man. Lady Caroline has been sitting here in all her dirt with us, but when you were announced, she flew to beautify herself … From that moment, for more than nine months, he almost lived at Melbourne House. It was then the centre of all gaiety, at least, in appearance … All the bon ton of London assembled here every day. There was nothing so fashionable, Byron contrived to sweep them all away." These utterances, reported with stenographic exactness, give an excellent idea of the fashionable life of the day in London.

everything in her power to break it off. Lady Caroline was at last persuaded to go to Ireland on a visit. Byron wrote a farewell letter to her, of which she allowed Lady Morgan to make a copy—a letter which is typical of his style in his immature years, and in which no one with any knowledge of the human heart will find the language of love. It reminds us of Hamlet's ambiguous letter to Ophelia.

> If tears which you saw, and know I am not apt to shed—if the agitation in which I parted from you—agitation which you must have perceived through the whole of this most nervous affair, did not commence until the moment of leaving you approached—if all I have said and done, and am still but too ready to say and do, have not sufficiently proved what my real feelings are, and must ever be towards you, my love, I have no other proof to offer … Is there anything in earth or heaven that would have made me so happy as to have made you mine long ago? You know I would with pleasure give up all here and beyond the grave for you, and in refraining from this, must my motives be misunderstood? I care not who knows this, what use is made of it—it is to you and to you only that they are, *yourself*, I was and am yours freely and entirely to obey, to honour, love, and fly with you when, where, and how yourself *might* and *may* determine.

It will surprise no one to learn that a few months later Byron himself put an end to the *liaison*; his love had never been anything but the kind of reflected love which imitates in a mirror all the motions of the flame, without fire of its own. Meeting Byron at a ball soon afterwards, Lady Caroline, maddened by his indifference, seized the first sharp thing that she could lay hold of—some say a pair of scissors, others a broken glass—and tried to cut her throat with it. After the ineffectual attempt at suicide, she (according to Countess Guiccioli) made "the most incredible promises" to a young nobleman on condition that he would challenge and kill the faithless one; nevertheless she herself soon called at her quondam lover's apartments, "by no means with the intention of cutting either her own throat or his." He was not at home. The words which she wrote on a title-page of a book she found on his table, inspired the epigram:

"Remember thee!" which is to be found amongst Byron's poems.

Pining for revenge, Lady Caroline now seized her pen and wrote the novel, *Glenarvon*, which came out at the most unfortunate moment possible for Byron, namely, just after his wife had left him, and was one of the most active ingredients in the ferment of public disapproval. The book, which has as its motto two lines from *The Corsair*:—

> He left a name to all succeeding times,
> Link'd with one virtue and a thousand crimes,

pictures Byron as a perfect demon of dissimulation and wickedness, endowed with all his hero's worst characteristics. But, possibly by way of excuse for her own conduct, the authoress has not been able to resist giving him some admirable and attractive qualities. One passage runs:

> Had he betrayed in his manner that freedom, that familiarity so offensive in men, but yet so frequent amongst them, she would have shuddered; but from what was she to fly? Not from the gross adulation, or the easy, flippant protestations to which all women are, soon or late, accustomed; but from a respect at once refined and flattering, an attention devoted even to her least wishes, yet without appearing subservient a gentleness and sweetness as rare as they were fascinating; and these combined with all the powers of imagination, vigour of intellect, and brilliancy of wit which none ever before possessed in so eminent a degree.

In 1817, when Byron was living in Venice, an Italian translation of *Glenarvon* was sent to press there. The censor refused to sanction its publication until he had ascertained if Lord Byron had any objections. Byron assured him that he had none. Only once again in the biography of Lord Byron is mention made of Lady Caroline Lamb. As the funeral procession following his corpse (which had been brought home from Greece) was slowly making its way from London to Newstead, it was met by a lady and gentleman on horseback. The lady inquired who it was that was to be buried. When she heard, she fell fainting from her horse. She was the authoress of *Glenarvon*.

Byron's giddy, wild London career was arrested by the most fateful event of his life—his marriage.

Life, as he had lived it, had not inspired him with much respect for woman; but the kind of woman he loved was the devoted, self-sacrificing creature whom he delighted in portraying in his poems. The woman whom chance made his wife had a strong, obstinate English character. Miss Anne Isabella Milbanke was the only child of a rich baronet. Byron was attracted by her simplicity and modesty, and tempted by the prospect of restoring Newstead with the help of her fortune. She annoyed him by refusing his hand when he first offered it to her, but fascinated him again by soon afterwards beginning a friendly correspondence with him of her own accord. In course of time she returned a favourable answer to a letter of proposal which he had written in an unwarrantably frivolous mood, and sent because a friend who read it thought it a pity that such "a pretty letter" should not go.

From motives which were, one and all, bad— motives of vanity, motives of vulgar aggrandisement—Byron rushed into a marriage which did not end worse than might have been expected. His mood during his engagement was a comparatively cheerful one. He writes to a lady friend:

Of course I am very much in love, and as silly as all single gentlemen must be in that sentimental situation.

And to another friend he writes:

I am now the happiest of mortals, for I became engaged a week ago. Yesterday I met young F., also the happiest of mortals, for he too is engaged.

So childish are all the letters written at this time that, if we believe them, we must suppose Byron's only serious trouble to have been the necessity of being married in a blue coat. However, as the wedding-day approached, he became ever more ill at ease; the relations between his parents had early inoculated him with a dread of marriage. His feelings during the wedding ceremony he has described in *The Dream*. He told Medwin that he trembled and gave wrong answers.

"The treacle-moon," as Byron calls it, did not run its course unshadowed by clouds. Two months after his marriage he writes to Moore from the country, where he and his wife were staying with her parents:

I am in a state of sameness and stagnation, totally occupied in consuming the fruits, and sauntering, and playing dull games at cards, and yawning, and trying to read old Annual Registers and the daily papers, and gathering shells on the shore, and watching the growth of stunted gooseberry bushes in the garden.

A few days later he writes:

I have been very comfortable here—listening to that d—d monologue which elderly gentlemen call conversation, and in which my pious father-in-law repeats himself every evening—save one, when he played upon the fiddle. However, they have been very kind and hospitable ... Bell is in health and unvaried good-humour and behaviour.

Pegasus was beginning to feel the yoke gall. However, the young couple presently went to London, where they lived in great style, keeping carriages and horses, and entertaining sumptuously, until Byron's creditors began to push their claims. Lady Byron's dowry of £10,000 disappeared like dew in sunshine, quickly followed by £8000, to which Byron had lately fallen heir. Things became so bad that he had to sell his library. In order to prevent this sale, Murray, his publisher, offered him £1500 as remuneration for his writings; but Byron's false pride led him to return the draft torn in pieces. Eight executions followed on each other in as many months; the very beds were seized at last.

Such was the position of affairs when, in December 1815, Lady Byron gave birth to her daughter Ada.

The spoiled young heiress had, of course, never dreamt that such experiences awaited her. The married life of the couple was at first by no means unhappy. They drove out together, and the young wife waited patiently in the carriage while her husband paid calls. She wrote letters for him and copied out poems, among others *The Bride of Corinth*. But there had very soon been small misunderstandings. Lady Byron seems to have been in the habit of constantly interrupting her husband with questions and remarks when he was writing, thereby giving occasion to outbursts of temper which she considered most unseemly. She had had no experience of such passionate violence and eccentric behaviour as she was soon to witness.

On one occasion she saw Byron, when in a passion, throw his watch into the fire and break it to pieces with the poker; on another, in fun or by accident, he fired off a pistol in her room. Ere long, too, she was suffering the pangs of jealousy. She knew of his notoriety as the hero of many amours, and knew more particularly about his connection with Lady Caroline Lamb, who was her own near relative. Byron had, unfortunately for his domestic peace, become a member of the Committee of Management of Drury Lane Theatre, and his correct lady was much perturbed by the business relations with actresses, singers, and ballet-dancers which this entailed. A person in her service (described by Lord Byron in *A Sketch*) began to act the spy, ransacking Byron's drawers and reading his letters. And there is yet another disagreeable matter, which we shall notice later.

With her husband's consent, the young wife, about a month after the child's birth, left the unsettled and unhappy home, and went on a visit to her parents. But hardly had she arrived before her father intimated to Byron that she would not return to him. While on the journey she had written a letter to him (now in print) which begins: "Dear Duck," and ends quite as affectionately. Byron's surprise may be imagined. He replied to his father-in-law that in this matter he could not acknowledge paternal authority, and must hear from his wife herself. Her communication was to the same effect. In 1830 Lady Byron publicly affirmed that she had written to her husband as affectionately as she did, in the belief that he was insane; and that if this idea of hers had proved to be the correct one, she would have borne everything as his faithful wife, but that in no other case could she have continued to live with him.

In a fragment of a novel, written by Byron in 1817, we have a corroboration of this assertion:—

A few days after, she set out for Aragon, with my son, on a visit to her father and mother. I did not accompany her immediately, having been in Aragon before ... During her journey I received a very affectionate letter from Donna Josepha, apprising me of the welfare of herself and my son. On her arrival at the château, I received another, still more affectionate, pressing me, in very fond and rather foolish terms, to join her immediately. As I was preparing to set out from Seville, I received a third—this was from her father, Don José di Cardozo, who requested me, in the politest manner, to dissolve our marriage. I answered him, with equal politeness, that I would do no such thing. A fourth letter arrived—it was from Donna Josepha, in which she informed me that her father's letter was written by her particular desire. I requested the reason by return of post: she replied, by express, that as reason had nothing to do with the matter, it was unnecessary to give any— but that she was an injured and excellent woman. I then inquired why she had written to me the two preceding affectionate letters, requesting me to come to Aragon. She answered, that was because she believed me out of my senses—that, being unfit to take care of myself, I had only to set out on this journey alone, and, making my way without difficulty to Don José di Cardozo's, I should there have found the tenderest of wives and— a strait-waistcoat.

When it became known that Byron's wife had left him, a sudden and complete change in the attitude of the public towards him took place. He had awakened one morning after the publication of *Childe Harold* to find himself famous; now came a morning when he awoke to find himself infamous, regarded by society as an outlaw.

Chief among the causes of this revulsion was envy—not that envy in the hearts of the gods which the ancients regarded as the cause of the downfall of the great—but foul, base envy in the breasts of his fellow-men. He stood so high; he was so great; with all his faults he had never sunk to the level of vulgar, mechanical respectability; confident in his powers and the favour of fortune, he had never deigned to seek friends who could protect him, or heeded how many enemies he made. These latter had long been innumerable. Chief among the envious were his literary rivals; and amongst all the many species of envy, the envy of authors is one of the most venomous. He had derided them, had called them the writers of a decadent period, had taken from some the name they had won, and made it impossible for others to win a name—why should he be admired and idolised whilst they were in vain arranging their locks for the reception of a wreath which never came? What joy to be able to tear him from the golden throne of fame and besmirch him with the mud in which they themselves stood!

He had long been suspected and secretly hated by the orthodox in religion and politics. The couple of stanzas in *Childe Harold* which venture in the most cautious terms to express a doubt that we shall meet our friends again after death, had been greeted with a cry of—heresy! and a whole book, *Anti-Byron*, had been written against them. The two verses to the Princess Charlotte, which, under the title, *Lines to a Lady Weeping*, were appended to the first edition of *The Corsair*, and in which the poet condoles with the daughter on the occasion of her father, the Prince Regent's, desertion of the Liberal side in politics, had set the whole Tory party violently against him. But hitherto he had been protected by his magic influence over men's minds as by an invisible coat of mail. This unfortunate episode in his private life offered a weak point, against which his enemies diverted the full force of public opinion.

The life led by Lady Byron and her family was the life on which English public opinion has set the seal of its peculiar approbation; and it was easy to convince the public that the man whom such a wife felt obliged to leave must indeed be a monster. Rumours began to spread; the slanders once conceived and brought forth, developed feet to walk on, wings to fly with, and swelled as they flew. Their voices rose from a whisper to a cry, from a cry to a deafening roar. Who does not know that concerted piece in the production of which baseness and stupidity collaborate, and during the performance of which ignorance sings in chorus with conscious villainy, whilst spite heightens the effect by the contribution of its most piercing trills!

Envy in this case entered the service of hypocrisy, and took its wages. Refined hypocrisy was, far on into the nineteenth century—as long, namely, as the period of religious reaction lasted—a social power, the authority of which differed from that of the Inquisitional tribunals of the sixteenth century only in the means it employed, not in the reach and efficacy of these means. It wrought through public opinion, and public opinion had become what Byron calls it in *Childe Harold*,

> an omnipotence—whose veil
> Mantles the earth with darkness, until right
> And wrong are accidents, and men grow pale
> Lest their own judgments should become too bright,
> And their free thoughts be crimes, and earth have
> too much light.

As for hypocrisy, he felt incapable of doing justice to it unaided. "Oh for a forty-parson power!" he cries in *Don Juan*:—

> Oh for a *forty-parson power* to chant
> Thy praise, Hypocrisy! Oh for a hymn
> Loud as the virtues thou dost loudly vaunt,
> Not practise! Oh for trump of cherubim!

Such a state of matters was inevitable at a period which has so much in common with the age when the ancient religions and theories of life were in process of dissolution; a period when an old theological theory of the universe and of life, everywhere undermined and riddled by science, and unable to support itself by its own inherent truth, was obliged to cling to the conventional morality of the upper classes, which it made as rigid as possible in order to have a support in it; a period when ecclesiastical authority and narrow-minded social conservatism, both in a tottering condition, were endeavouring to uphold each other. Taking a bird's-eye view of the psychological history of Europe during the first two decades of the century, it actually seems to us as if the whole edifice of hypocrisy, the foundations of which were laid in the writings of the French *émigrés*, which rose steadily in those of the German Romanticists, and towered to a giddy height during the French Reaction, now suddenly fell on the head of one man.

Macaulay, in his essay on Moore's *Life of Byron*, writing on this subject, says:—

> We know no spectacle so ridiculous as the British public in one of its periodical fits of morality. In general, elopements, divorces, and family quarrels, pass with little notice. We read the scandal, talk about it for a day, and forget it. But once in six or seven years our virtue becomes outrageous. We cannot suffer the laws of religion and decency to be violated. We must make a stand against vice. We must teach libertines that the English people appreciate the importance of domestic ties. Accordingly some unfortunate man, in no respect more depraved than hundreds whose offences have been treated with lenity, is singled out as an expiatory sacrifice. If he has children, they are to be taken from him. If he has a profession, he is to be driven from it.

He is cut by the higher orders, and hissed by the lower. He is, in truth, a sort of whipping-boy, by whose vicarious agonies all the other transgressors of the same class are, it is supposed, sufficiently chastised. We reflect very complacently on our own severity, and compare with great pride the high standard of morals established in England with the Parisian laxity. At length our anger is satiated. Our victim is ruined and heart-broken. And our virtue goes quietly to sleep for seven years more.

If the causes of Byron's downfall were of a complex nature, the means were simple enough. It was compassed by the Press, the only effective instrument in such cases. Several of the papers and magazines had taken the opportunity to spread slanders about him when criticising his verses to the Princess Charlotte; and more than one of them periodically calumniated him. Now they were all at liberty to discuss and attack his private life freely, thanks to the anonymity which, in spite of the want of naturalness and the corruption it entails, still prevails in the English Press. What anonymity really means is simply this, that the paltriest scribbler, who is hardly fit to hold the pen with which he writes his lies, is enabled to put the trumpet of moral public opinion to his lips, and let the voice of injured virtue resound in thousands of homes. Nor is it enough that the one anonymous writer should be able to constitute himself the voice of the public in the thousands of copies of one newspaper; he can assume hundreds of forms, can write with all kinds of fanciful signatures, and in a dozen different newspapers and magazines. A single scribbler would have sufficed to provide the whole Press with base attacks on a man outlawed by public opinion; it is easy, then, to imagine the number that were made on Byron, whose enemies were legion. Among the names given him by the Press he himself remembered Nero, Apicius, Caligula, Heliogabalus, and Henry VIII.—that is to say, he was accused of inhuman cruelty, of insane brutality, of animal and unnatural lust; he was painted with all the colours which vileness smears on its palette. The most terrible of all the accusations was that which even then went the round of the newspapers, and which sullied the fair name of the being dearest to him—the accusation of incest. And to all this he could not answer a word! He could not fight with the mire that bespattered him.

Slanders sped from mouth to mouth. When Mrs. Mardyn, the Drury Lane actress, made her first appearance after the divorce, she was hissed off the stage, because of the perfectly groundless report of a *liaison* between her and Byron, to whom, as a matter of fact, she had only spoken twice. He himself could not appear on the streets without danger. On his way to the House of Lords, where his presence was ignored, he was insulted by a respectable crowd.

Defence or retort being impossible, no course was left him, proud as he was, but to bow his head and go. He writes:

> I felt that, if what was whispered, and muttered, and murmured, was true, I was unfit for England; if false, England was unfit for me.

On the 25th of April, 1816, he set sail, never to return alive.

It is from this moment that Byron's true greatness dates. The blow struck by the *Edinburgh Review* had roused him, for the first time, to intellectual activity. This new blow made of him a knight. There is no comparison possible between what Byron wrote before, and what he wrote after, the event which he himself regarded as his greatest misfortune. It was a misfortune sent him by the genius of History, to snatch him from the unmanning influence of idolisation, to sever the enfeebling connection between him and that society and social spirit against which it was his historic mission to arouse, with more fortune and more power than any other individual, the hostility which was its undoing.

XIX

BYRON: HIS SELF-ABSORPTION

WHEN HE HAD BECOME FOR THE SECOND time a homeless and solitary pilgrim, Byron began to occupy himself again with the poem of travel in which his youthful sentiments had found expression. He added the Third and Fourth Cantos to *Childe Harold*. He turned back and felt the youthful feelings once again. But what breadth and depth they had gained in the interval! The chord struck in the First and Second Cantos was composed of three notes—the note of solitariness, the note of melancholy, and the note of freedom. Each one of these had become far clearer and more resonant.

Throughout the first half of the work it is the feeling of solitariness which produces the love of nature. "To sit on rocks, to muse o'er flood and fell," to climb the trackless mountain and lean over the foaming waterfall, alone, was not solitariness, but communion with nature; true solitariness was to wander amidst "the crowd, the hum, the shock of men," unloving and unloved. (*Childe Harold*, ii. 25, 26, 27.) The outbursts in the stanzas referred to are evoked by remembrances of the poet's childhood, spent in the beautiful mountain districts of Scotland, or of his visit to the hermit's home on "lonely Athos." This was still a love of the solitude of nature which resembled Wordsworth's, and which was based upon fear of an unknown, strange world of men and women. The difference between Wordsworth's and Byron's feeling was no more than this—that Wordsworth dwelt silently on the natural impression, in the manner of the countryman and the landscape painter, while Byron seized it with the longing, nervous ardour of the townsman; and, moreover, that Wordsworth loved nature best in her quiet moods, Byron in her wrath. (*Childe Harold*, ii. 37.)

In the second half of the work the character of the poet's solitariness has changed. There is a marked difference between the desire for solitary communion with nature which Harold felt as an inexperienced youth, and that which he felt as a man, at the end of his first circumnavigation of the world of men and things. It was now no longer fear of human beings, but disgust with them, which drove him to take refuge with nature. Society, the best society of a great metropolis, which to the untrained eye seemed so humane, so right-thinking, so refined and chivalrous, had turned its wrong side towards him—and the wrong side is interesting, but not beautiful. He had learned how much friendship the ruined man may reckon on, had learned that the only force which he who is making plans for his future can exactly calculate is the self-love of his fellow-men, with its consequences. So he withdrew into himself again; and the poetry he wrote at this time is not for men of a sociable nature. But the man who has had even a short experience of what it is to turn his back on his fellow-men—who in his desire to escape from them has left his home, his country, in search of a new earth and new skies—who in the solitudes of his choice has felt the sight of an approaching human being equivalent to a foul spot on his pure, free horizon—in the souls of this man and his like, Byron's lyric outbursts will find an echo.

Childe Harold is a solitary. He has learned that he is "the most unfit of men to herd with man," because he is unable "to submit his thoughts to others … to yield dominion of his mind to spirits against whom his own rebelled." But,

> Where rose the mountains, there to him were
> friends;
> Where roll'd the ocean, thereon was his home.
> .   .   .   .
> The desert, forest, cavern, breaker's foam,
> Were unto him companionship; they spake
> A mutual language, clearer than the tome
> Of his land's tongue, which he would oft forsake
> For Nature's pages glass'd by sunbeams on the lake.

Amongst men he droops like a wild-born falcon with clipt wing. But in his case, to fly from, is not to hate, mankind. It is not discontent or defiance which keeps his "mind deep in its fountain," but fear lest it should "overboil in the hot throng," where in a moment

> We may plunge our years
> In fatal penitence, and in the blight
> Of our own soul, turn all our blood to tears.

He feels that it is better to be alone, and thus to become a portion of what surrounds him. High mountains are "a feeling" to him, but the hum of human cities is a torture. The mountain, the sky, and the sea are a part of him, and he is a part of them, and to love them is his purest happiness. In solitude he is least alone; then his soul is conscious of infinity, a truth which purifies it from self. Harold has not loved the world, nor has it loved him. He is proud of not having "flattered its rank breath," nor bowed the knee to its idols, nor smiled hypocritically, nor echoed the cries of the crowd. He was *among* them, but not *of* them. But he desires that the world and he should part fair foes. "I do believe," he says,

> Though I have found them not, that there may be
> Words which are things—hopes which will not
>   deceive,
> And virtues which are merciful ...
> That two, or one, are almost what they seem."[13]

The feeling of solitariness gradually becomes the feeling of *melancholy*. This note, too, had been struck in the first two cantos; but their melancholy was nothing but the discontent of youth. With a wasted youth behind him, he had stood, like a phlegmatically mournful Hamlet, at the grave of Achilles, declaiming, with a skull in his hand, on the worthlessness of life and fame—this young poet who had not yet tasted the sweetness of celebrity, and who in reality hungered for nothing so much as for that very fame which, with so much argumentative philosophy, he feigned to condemn and despise. Now he has tasted it, and learned how little nourishment is to be derived from such food.

His heart is:

> Even as a broken mirror, which the glass
> In every fragment multiplies; and makes
> A thousand images of one that was,
> The same and still the more, the more it breaks.

In the depth of his dejection he turns to the element in nature which, by its contrast with his present mood, solaces his sufferings—the sea, the free, open sea, upon whose mane he had laid his hand as a boy, and which knows him as the horse knows his rider. He loves the sea because it is unconquerable, because time cannot even write a wrinkle on its brow, and it rolls now as it rolled at the dawn of creation. But everything in nature reminds him of suffering and warfare. The peal of distant thunder is to him an alarm-bell, "the knoll of what in me is sleepless—if I rest." Even the beautiful, calm lake of Nemi does not remind him of anything peaceful and sweet; he calls it "calm as cherished hate." (iv. 173.)

His melancholy becomes actually choleric. Could he breathe all his passion "into *one* word, and that one word were Lightning," he would speak. "Anything but rest!" is his watchword. "Quiet to quick bosoms is a hell." There is a fire in the soul which, once kindled, is quenchless, and the flames of which rise ever higher and wilder; there is a fever which is fatal to all whom it attacks:

> This makes the madmen who have made men mad
> By their contagion; Conquerors and Kings,
> Founders of sects and systems, to whom add
> Sophists, Bards, Statesmen, all unquiet things
> Which stir too strongly the soul's secret springs,
> And are themselves the fools to those they fool;
> Envied, yet how unenviable! what stings
> Are theirs! One breast laid open were a school
> Which would unteach mankind the lust to shine
>   or rule.

> Their breath is agitation, and their life
> A storm whereon they ride, to sink at last,
> And yet so nursed and bigoted to strife,
> That should their days, surviving perils past,
> Melt to calm twilight, they feel overcast
> With sorrow and supineness, and so die;
> Even as a flame unfed, which runs to waste
> With its own flickering, or a sword laid by,
> Which eats into itself, and rusts ingloriously.

---

[13] *Childe Harold*, iii. 114.

And in a still more despairing mood Harold cries:

> We wither from our youth, we gasp away—
> Sick—sick; unfound the boon—unslaked the thirst,
> Though to the last, in verge of our decay,
> Some phantom lures, such as we sought at first—
> But all too late—so are we doubly curst.
> Love, fame, ambition, avarice—'tis the same,
> Each idle—and all ill—and none the worst—
> For all are meteors with a different name,
> And Death the sable smoke where vanishes the flame.
>
> .   .   .   .
>
> Our life is a false nature—'tis not in
> The harmony of things—this hard decree,
> This uneradicable taint of sin,
> This boundless upas, this all-blasting tree,
> Whose root is earth, whose leaves and branches be
> The skies which rain their plagues on men like dew—
> Disease, death, bondage—all the woes we see,
> And worse, the woes we see not. .   .   .

In the First Canto of *Childe Harold* we already find the *love of freedom* (the third note in the chord struck by the poem) exalted as the one force capable of emancipating from the despair with which the universal misery (the *Weltschmerz*, as the Germans call it) has overwhelmed the soul. It has this power because it provides a practical task. During his first visit to Portugal, Childe Harold exclaimed: "Oh, that such hills upheld a free-born race!" And to the Spaniards he cried:

> Awake, ye sons of Spain! awake! Advance!
> Lo, Chivalry, your ancient goddess, cries.

And it was in the course of his first tour, too, that he thus apostrophised the subjugated Greeks, who went on hoping for help from other nations:—

> Hereditary bondsmen! know ye not
> Who would be free themselves must strike the blow?
> By their right arms the conquest must be wrought?
> Will Gaul or Muscovite redress ye? No!
> True, they may lay your proud despoilers low,
> But not for you will Freedom's altars flame.
>
> .   .   .   .
>
> When riseth Lacedemon's hardihood,
> When Thebes Epaminondas rears again,
> When Athens' children are with hearts endued,
> When Grecian mothers shall give birth to men,
> Then may'st thou be restored; but not till then.

But his love of liberty at that time was of a purely political nature; it was the free-born Englishman's indignation at seeing other nations unable to shake off a foreign yoke to which his own nation would never have dreamt of submitting.

Now he has learned what liberty in the wide, full, universal meaning of the word is. Now he feels that free *thought* is the first essential requisite of all spiritual life.

> Yet let us ponder boldly—'tis a base
> Abandonment of reason to resign
> Our right of thought—our last and only place
> Of refuge; this, at least, shall still be mine:
> Though from our birth the faculty divine
> Is chain'd and tortured—cabin'd, cribb'd, confined,
> And bred in darkness, lest the truth should shine
> Too brightly on the unprepared mind,
> The beam pours in, for time and skill will couch
> the blind.

And it is his intention not merely to ponder, but to act. Invoking Time, the great avenger, whom he reminds that he has borne the hatred of the world with calm pride—and he has experienced all its varieties of hatred,

> From mighty wrongs to petty perfidy,
>
> .   .   .   .   .   .
>
> From the loud roar of foaming calumny
> To the small whisper of the as paltry few,
> And subtler venom of the reptile crew—

he concludes with the prayer: "Let me not have worn this iron in my soul in vain!"

Now, his personal woes shrink into nothing when he beholds the gigantic ruins of Rome; and, like the Sulpicius with whose feelings Chateaubriand endowed the hero of *Les Martyrs*, he feels the insignificance of his fate compared with that which has swept away the cities of Greece. He writes:—

> Oh Rome! my country! city of the soul!
> The orphans of the heart must turn to thee,
> Lone mother of dead empires! and control
> In their shut breasts their petty misery.
>
> .   .   .   .
>
> Wandering in youth, I traced the path of him,
> The Roman friend of Rome's least mortal mind,
> The friend of Tully.

And when, not satisfied with liberty of thought alone, he turns his attention to practical matters and occupies himself with the great political struggles of the day, he does not content himself with repeating the old invocations to the departed, or with crying to Venice that she has drowned the glory and honour of centuries in the mire of slavery, and that it would be better for her to be whelm'd beneath the waves. No, he boldly attacks the mighty, the victors of Waterloo, whom he scornfully calls "the apes of him who humbled once the proud"; and then passes from the outward, political aspect of the great European conflicts, to their inner, social significance.

To all appearance, he says, France has uprooted old prejudices, and laid in ruins "things which grew, breathed from the birth of time," only to see dungeons and thrones rebuilt upon the same foundation. "*But this will not endure.*" Mankind have at last felt their strength. And even though France "got drunk with blood to vomit crime,"

> Yet, Freedom! yet thy banner, torn, but flying,
> Streams like the thunderstorm *against* the wind;
> Thy trumpet voice, though broken now and dying,
> The loudest still the tempest leaves behind;
> Thy tree hath lost its blossoms, and the rind,
> Chopp'd by the axe, looks rough and little worth,
> But the sap lasts—and still the seed we find
> Sown deep, even in the bosom of the North;
> So shall a better spring less bitter fruit bring forth.

And of himself the poet writes:—

> But I have lived, and have not lived in vain:
> My mind may lose its force, my blood its fire,
> And my frame perish even in conquering pain;
> But there is that within me which shall tire
> Torture and Time, and breathe when I expire,
> Something unearthly, which they deem not of,
> Like the remember'd tone of a mute lyre.

Thus do the three chief feelings expressed in this beautiful poem—solitariness, melancholy, and love of freedom—gradually become one greater feeling; the mind of the poet widens and deepens with each canto. Wordsworth had identified his Ego with England; Scott and Moore had given the feelings of Scotland and Ireland expression in their poetry; but Byron's Ego represents universal humanity; its sorrows and hopes are those of all mankind. After this Ego has, in manly, energetic style, withdrawn into itself and lived for a time absorbed in its solitary grief, that grief widens into compassion for all the sufferings and sorrows of humanity; the hard, selfish crust of the Ego is broken, and there issues forth the ardent love of liberty, to encompass and to elevate the poet's whole generation. Now his mind is attuned to worship, and he cries:—

> Not vainly did the early Persian make
> His altar the high places and the peak
> Of earth-o'ergazing mountains …
> .   .   .   .   Come and compare
> Columns and idol-dwellings, Goth or Greek,
> With Nature's realms of worship, earth and air,
> Nor fix on fond abodes to circumscribe thy prayer.

XX

BYRON: THE REVOLUTIONARY SPIRIT

FTER VISITING THE BATTLE-FIELD OF Waterloo, Byron went, by way of the Rhine, to Switzerland, where he spent several months, residing most of the time in the neighbourhood of Geneva. In a boarding-house there, he for the first time met Shelley. Shelley, who was Byron's junior by four years, had sent him, at the time of its publication, a copy of *Queen Mab*; but the letter accompanying the book had miscarried, and no further communication had passed between them, Shelley had arrived at Geneva a fortnight before Byron, accompanied by Mary Godwin and her step-sister, Miss Jane Clairmont, who had always passionately admired Byron. His illegitimate daughter Allegra was the fruit of the brief connection between him and this young lady.

Intercourse with Shelley produced on Byron's mind some of the strongest, deepest impressions which it was capable of receiving. The first great impression was that made by Shelley's personality and view of life. In him Byron for the first time came into contact with a man of a perfectly modern and perfectly emancipated mind. In spite of his genius for assimilating everything that harmonised with his own nature, it was but a half education, in philosophy as in literature, which Byron had received; and he had hitherto, been led by sympathies rather than convictions. Now Shelley, glowing with the enthusiasm of an apostle, his doubts long since disposed of, a true priest of humanism, came across his path. The dissipated life of London society, and the pressing burden of his private misfortunes, had allowed Byron neither tranquillity of mind nor leisure to reflect on the problems of existence or on the reformation of humanity; he had been too much occupied with himself. Now, at the moment in his literary career when his Ego was beginning to expand, he was brought into contact with a spirit which baptized with fire. He gladly welcomed the new influence;

and in much of what he now wrote it is plainly perceptible. The numerous pantheistic outbursts in the Third Canto of *Childe Harold* are undoubtedly, one and all, the fruit of conversations with Shelley; worthy of special attention is the beautiful passage (iii. ioo) in which everything in Nature is assumed to be a manifestation of "undying Love"—an expression of Shelley's theory of love and beauty being the mysterious powers which uphold the world. In one of the notes in his journal, Byron at this time goes so far in his Shelley-derived pantheism as to write:

> The feeling with which all around Clarens and the opposite rocks of Meillerie is invested, is of a still higher and more comprehensive order than the mere sympathy with individual passion; it is a sense of the existence of love in its most extended and sublime capacity, and of our own participation of its good and of its glory: it is the great principle of the universe, which is there more condensed, but not less manifested; and of which, though knowing ourselves a part, we lose our individuality, and mingle in the beauty of the whole.

Shelley's influence is also traceable in the spirit scenes in *Manfred*, and very specially in the third act of the drama, which was re-written by his advice. And as to *Cain*, even if Shelley, as he affirms, had no actual share in the writing of the work, it certainly would not have been what it is if Byron had never known him.

The two poets saw Chillon and all its beautiful surroundings in company; and Byron received the second great impression which was to bear fruit in his poetry—the impression of the Alps. Coming from the confinement and close atmosphere of the London drawing-rooms, it was a relief to him to let his eye rest on the eternal snow, and the giant peaks that tower sky-high above the haunts of men.

His poetic forerunner, Chateaubriand, hated the Alps; their grandeur had an oppressive effect on his vanity; Byron felt at home among them.

Manfred, which derives its truest claim to admiration from its matchlessness as an Alpine landscape, was a direct result of the impressions of nature received at this time. Taine let himself be tempted to use the strong expression, that Byron's Alpine Spirits in *Manfred* are only stage gods; but Taine, when he wrote this, did not himself know Switzerland.

Nowhere else do circumstances in the same degree incline the mind to the personification of nature. Even the ordinary traveller feels the temptation. I remember standing one evening on the summit of the Righi, looking down on the beautiful lakes at the foot of the mountain, and the vapoury clouds which were driving across them, quite close to their surface. Suddenly, far away on the horizon, a little solid white cloud appeared. By the time it had reached Pilatus, a minute later, it was an enormous vapoury mass. With frightful speed it rushed onwards, covering the whole sky with the league-wide flaps of its mantle. Sinking down towards the lakes, it enveloped the mountain peaks, rode along the ridges, filled the hollows; then, spreading itself out still wider, t mounted in circles like smoke towards the sky, and sank like lead over the towns and villages, effacing every colour, and turning the whole into one monotonous expanse of grey. The white of the snow, the green of the trees, the thousand gleams and colours of the sunlit clouds were deluged and gone in one moment. The eye, which had but a second before been wandering at will over the immeasurable expanse now, irresistibly attracted, gazed steadfastly at the shapeless mass, which, tearing through the sky with the force of a sphere in its earliest stage, rapidly approached the beholder. It was like the hosts of heaven, like hundreds of thousands of ethereal riders, sweeping onwards in closed ranks upon winged, silent horses, and, more irresistible than any earthly army, tracklessly effacing everything behind them, like the hordes of Asia or Attila's Huns. A Scandinavian could not but think of the ride of the Valkyries. The moment the cloud eached the Righi, the watchers there began to lose sight of each other; first one, then another, disappeared from the view of his companions; the mist slung itself in a clammy, tight embrace round each one, closing his mouth and weighing on his breast.

Natural phenomena of this description suggested the apparitions which appear to Manfred. Passage after passage from Byron's journal is incorporated in his poem. Not unfrequently the entries in their original, careless form are fully as effective as when transcribed in verse.

Arrived at the Grindelwald; dined; mounted again, and rode to the higher glacier—like *a frozen hurricane*. (In Manfred, for the sake of the verse—"a tumbling tempest's foam, frozen in a moment.") Starlight, beautiful, but a devil of a path! ... A little lightning; but the whole of the day as fine in point of weather as the day on which Paradise was made. Passed *whole woods of withered pines, all withered*; trunks stripped and barkless, branches lifeless; done by a single winter—their appearance reminded me of me and my family.

All these expressions occur, with slight alterations, in the poem.

But the time Shelley and Byron spent together, profitable and enjoyable as it was, would have been happier but for the behaviour of some of their fellow-countrymen, whose curiosity led them to dog the footsteps and spy the actions of the two poets. English tourists had the incredible impertinence to force their way into Byron's house. When a stop was put to this, they stood with telescopes on the shore or on the road; they looked over the garden-wall; and hotel waiters were bribed, as the Venetian gondoliers afterwards were, to communicate all that went on. The first report set in circulation was, that Byron and Shelley lived in "promiscuous intercourse" with two sisters; and, gossip by degrees making the two poets out to be incarnate devils, the reports gained steadily in repulsiveness. It consequently hardly surprises us to read that, one day at Madame de Staël's, when Byron was announced, a pious old English lady, Mrs. Hervey, the novel-writer, fainted when she heard the name, as if, says Byron, it had been "his Satanic majesty" himself who was appearing.

Our attempt to understand this actual fear of Byron's person, which to us appears so absurd, leads us to the consideration of the last great impression received by him during his stay by the Lake of Geneva, namely, that produced by his clear apprehension of the exact nature of a certain calumny which had been for some time in circulation in England, and also of the wide-spread belief in it. This was the same story which Mrs. Beecher Stowe in the sixties published to the world, as having been confidentially communicated to herself by Lady Byron, "whilst a heavenly brightness shone from that lady's ethereal countenance"—the story of the criminal relations between Lord Byron and his step-sister, Augusta Leigh. The assurance that such relations had existed became in course of time so firmly rooted in Lady Byron's mind that (as is proved by a work entitled *Medora Leigh*, published in 1869) she did not even shrink from telling Augusta's daughter, Medora, who applied to her for assistance when in difficulties, that she was not a daughter of Colonel Leigh, but of Lord Byron. Lady Byron at the same time promised Medora that she would always provide for her maintenance—a promise she did not keep.

At the time he left England, Byron had evidently known nothing, or as good as nothing, of this report. He had probably not read all the hostile newspaper articles. He himself writes that it was not till some time afterwards that he heard of all his enemies had done and said; and he blames his friends for having concealed various things from him. It was while he was in Switzerland that he learned everything. Knowing this, we understand the full meaning of the poetry addressed at that time to Augusta. In the Third Canto of *Childe Harold* we find the following stanza:—

And there was one soft breast, as hath been said,
Which unto his was bound by stronger ties
Than the Church links withal; and, though unwed,
That love was pure, and, far above disguise,
Had stood the test of mortal enmities
Still undivided, and cemented more
By peril, dreaded most in female eyes;
But this was firm, and from a foreign shore
Well to that heart might his these absent greetings
      pour!

The *Stanzas to Augusta* express similar sentiments; and the line, "Though slander'd, thou never couldst shake" (in the second of the poems to her), shows that she, too knew of the shameful rumours.

And now we also have the explanation of the sudden revulsion which occurred in Switzerland in Byron's feeling towards Lady Byron. In the days immediately following the separation he had written:

I do not believe that there ever was a better, or even a brighter, a kinder, or a more amiable and agreeable being than Lady B.,

and had laid the blame of everything on his own violence and inconsiderateness; but now he sees only the blemishes in her character; and it is while under the overpowering impression made by the accusation just alluded to, that he begins the ugly war upon a woman, which, if we did not know the circumstances, would seem utterly inexcusable, and draws the unflattering portrait of his wife as Donna Inez in the First Canto of *Don Juan*.

Decisive, and positively crushing, evidence against Lady Byron was produced in 1869, in the *Quarterly Review*. Seven letters and notes were printed, written after the separation by her to Mrs. Leigh, all brimming over with tenderness and assurances of affection. It is her "great comfort" that Mrs. Leigh is with Lord Byron:

Shall I still be your sister? I must resign my rights to be so considered; but I don't think that will make any difference in the kindness I have so uniformly experienced from you.

.   .   .   .   .

In this at least I am 'truth itself' when I say that whatsoever the situation may be, there is no one whose society is dearer to me, or can contribute more to my happiness. These feelings will not change under any circumstances ... Should you hereafter condemn me, I shall not love you the less.

Thus did Lady Byron write to the woman whom, after the lapse of many years, she accused as the guilty person who had driven her from her husband's house. This friendly correspondence between Lady Byron and Mrs. Leigh actually continues till Byron's death. His last unfinished letter begins with the words: "My dearest Augusta, I received a few days ago your and Lady Byron's report of Ada's health." And yet we are asked to believe that Lady Byron the whole time regarded Augusta, who continued to be the reconciling intermediary between the spouses, as the unnatural criminal who was one of the authors of the misfortune of her life. What a chaos of lies and insanity!

Insanity is the right word, for, as the *Quarterly Review* has remarked,

Lady Byron could at first account for her gifted husband's conduct on no hypothesis but insanity; and now, by a sort of Nemesis, there is no other hypothesis on which the charitable moralist can account for hers. But there is this marked difference in their maladies: he morbidly exaggerated his vices, and she her virtues; his monomania lay in being an impossible sinner, and hers in being an impossible saint … He in his mad moods did his best to blacken his own reputation, whilst her self-delusions invariably tended to damage the characters of all that were nearest and should have been dearest to her. Which was the more dangerous or less amiable delusion of the two?[14]

The last impression received by Byron in Switzerland was, then, the crushing one of this slander. His thoughts revolved round the story, and the artist in him was ever more fascinated by it. George Sand, in a letter to Sainte-Beuve, has, with a few rapid touches, described her nature, and the nature of the poet generally. She is writing about Jouffroy the philosopher, who has expressed a desire to be introduced to her, but of whom, as an extremely rigorous and unimaginative moralist, she is a little afraid. She remarks:

I have once or twice said to myself: Might it not be permissible to eat human flesh? You have said to yourself: People doubtless exist who think that it might be permissible to eat human flesh! Jouffroy has said to himself: Such an idea never occurred to any one, &c.

—a clever definition of the nature of the poet as compared with that of the observer and the moralist.

Byron was one of those who permit their imaginative and their reflective powers every possible experiment; he had a strong inclination to brood over, and let his fancy play with, what people in general fear and avoid. The well-known anecdote (which aroused such horror) of his exclaiming, with a knife in his hand:

I wish I knew what it feels like to have committed a murder,

means this and nothing more. There was the same fascination for him in thinking and working himself into the feeling of guilt which accompanies a criminal attachment, as there was in imagining the feelings which accompany a murder. His earliest heroes, such as the Giaour and Lara, have committed a mysterious murder; and, as is well known, Byron was promptly credited with the crime of his heroes. Even the aged Goethe allowed himself to be so far led astray by the gossip that reached his ears as to characterise (in his review of *Manfred*) as "extremely probable" the foolish tale of Byron's doings in Florence—where, as a matter of fact, he spent one afternoon. The story reported him to have had an intrigue there with a young married woman, who was, in consequence, killed by her husband—the husband in his turn being killed by Byron. Just as the public of that day saw evidence of Byron's murderous deeds in Lara's tragic mien, the public of our day have seen evidence of his incest in Manfred's despair and Cain's marriage with his sister. It is not surprising that Byron and Moore should have meditated writing an imaginary biography of Lord Byron, in which he was to seduce so many members of the one sex and murder so many of the other, that the scandal-mongers would be outbid and possibly silenced. The project was only relinquished from fear that the public might take the jest as sober earnest.

It is probable that the subject of love between brother and sister was one often discussed by Shelley and Byron in the course of their conversations, all the more probable from the circumstance that the younger poet's mind was also exercised by the unprofitable question. What incensed Byron more than anything else was the pious horror displayed by the orthodox Bible Christians, one article of whose faith it is that the human race, as descended from one man and woman, multiplied by means of marriage between brother and sister. Hence he lays emphasis in *Cain* on the circumstance that Cain and Adah are brother and sister, and makes Lucifer explain to Adah that *her* love for her brother is not a sin, though the same passion in her descendants will be; to which Adah very logically replies:

What is the sin which is not
Sin in itself? Can circumstance make sin
Or virtue?

[14] *Quarterly Review*, October 1869. Compare with Karl Elze's admirable work: *Lord Byron*, p. 179.

Manfred and *Cain* were the products of all the psychological elements which have now been indicated. *Manfred* is the less important of the two works. It does not bear the comparison with Goethe's *Faust* which it invites and which has been so often instituted. Goethe himself said that an interesting lecture might be given on the subject. They have since been given in abundance; there is more originality and talent in Taine's than in any other known to me.

At only one point does *Manfred* rise superior to *Faust*. To the critic there is no surer criterion of the value of the different parts of a work than the circumstance that, after a certain length of time, he remembers this or that part and has forgotten the rest. I know with certainty that, a year after I had read *Manfred*, all that I remembered of it was the scene in which, in the hour of his death, the hero, who has judged himself so severely, first repulses the Abbot and such comfort as he would fain give, and then with proud contempt dismisses from his presence the evil spirits with whom he has nothing in common, and to whom he has never given the slightest power over him. The difference between this man and Faust, who sells himself to Mephistopheles and falls on his knees before the Earth Spirit, is very striking. The English poet has had before his eyes a higher ideal of independent manhood than has the German; Byron's hero is a typical man, Goethe's a typical human being. Alone in death as in life, Manfred has no more communion with hell than he has with heaven. He is his own accuser and his own judge. This is Byron's manly ethical standpoint. Not till he reaches the lonely heights above the snow-line, where human weakness and pliability do not thrive, does his soul breathe freely. And the Alpine landscape is the natural, inevitable background for his hero whose stern wildness is akin to such scenes.

But in *Manfred* only the egoistic side of Byron's nature reveals itself. His wide human sympathies find full expression for the first time in *Cain*. *Cain* is Byron's confession of faith—that is to say, the confession of all his doubts and all his criticism. When we remember that he had neither, like Shelley and the great poets of Germany, attained by dint of thought to an emancipated, humanistic view of the world and life, nor, like the authors of our own days, had the advantage of being able to base his ideas and imaginings on the subject of the beliefs of the past and the present upon a groundwork of facts established by natural science

and scientific Biblical criticism, we cannot but marvel at the intellectual power and earnestness which he in this work brings to bear on the most vital problems of life.

As a private personage Byron was, undoubtedly, as much of the dilettante in his free-thought as in his politics. His admirable reasoning power revolted against belief in what was contrary to reason; but, like most of the great men at the beginning of the century—that is to say, before the remarkable development of religion and science which has taken place during its progress—he was sceptical and superstitious at one and the same time. As a child, religion had been made a weariness to him; his mother dragged him regularly to church, and he revenged himself when he was bored beyond all measure by pricking her with a pin. As a youth, he was roused to revolt by the rigid literal beliefs of the Church of England, as contained in its thirty-nine Articles; he wrote in his memorandum-book:

It is useless to tell me *not* to *reason*, but to *believe*. You might as well tell a man not to wake, but *sleep*."

The belief in eternal hell-fire was a subject of eternal merriment with him. He writes to Moore in 1822:

Do you remember Frederick the Great's answer to the remonstrance of the villagers whose curate preached against the eternity of hell's torments? It was thus:—'If my faithful subjects of Schrausenhaussen prefer being eternally damned, let them.'

And he horrified his fellow-countrymen by writing in *Don Juan*:

There's nought, no doubt, so much the spirit calms
As rum and true religion.

He disliked the clergy. Trelawny reports him to have said: "When did parsons patronise genius? If one of their black band dares to think for himself, he is drummed out or cast aside, like Sterne and Swift"; and Moore gives as one of his ejaculations:

These rascals of priests have done more harm to religion than all the unbelievers.

But, in spite of all his jests and jeers, his feeling was one of uncertainty. He dared not endorse the conclusions to which Shelley was led by his reflections; and he sent his little daughter to be educated in a convent, to withdraw her from the influence of the sceptical talk of Shelley and his wife. A beautiful and very characteristic letter from Shelley gives decisive evidence on the subject of Byron's uncertainty. He writes:

> Lord Byron has read me one or two letters of Moore to him, in which Moore speaks with great kindness of me; and of course I cannot but feel flattered by the approbation of a man, my inferiority to whom I am proud to acknowledge(!) Amongst other things, however, Moore seems to deprecate my influence on Lord Byron's mind on the subject of religion, and to attribute the tone assumed in *Cain* to my suggestion ... I think you know Moore. Pray assure him that I have not the smallest influence over Lord Byron in this particular; if I had, I certainly should employ it to eradicate from his great mind the delusions of Christianity, which, in spite of his reason, seem perpetually to recur, and to lie in ambush for the hours of sickness and distress. *Cain* was *conceived* many years ago, and begun before I saw him last year at Ravenna. How happy should I not be to attribute to myself, however indirectly, any participation in that immortal work!

Thus we see that Byron, the private individual, had by no means arrived at any definite conclusions on the great subjects which engage the mind of man. And we are consequently all the more impressed by the manner in which, in his poetry, his genius takes possession of him, and makes him great and victorious in his argument, directing his aim with absolute certainty to the vital points. In European literature, which in 1821 lay stifling in the clutches of orthodoxy, there was a perfect revolution when *Cain* appeared, like a herald of revolt; the only comparison possible is with the impression produced in the scientific world fourteen years later by Strauss's *Life of Jesus*. The great German poets had, in their liberal Hellenism, left the orthodox belief untouched. This less emancipated poet was confined in the cage of dogma, but was uneasily pacing round and round in it like an imprisoned wild animal, shaking at its bars.

Cain is not written with the haste of inspiration— is not a work that storms and thunders. In it Byron has succeeded in accomplishing what for passionate natures is the most difficult of all tasks—the accomplishment of which is, indeed, the supreme triumph of morality—he has *canalised* his passion, that is to say, caused its wild currents to fertilise. The play is a product of reflection—of the thought that burrows and mines, the acuteness that splits, the reasoning power that shivers. Here more than anywhere else is what Goethe makes Byron say of himself (as Euphorion in the Second Part of *Faust*) applicable—namely, that he has a distaste for what is easily won, and delights only in what he takes by force. But the whole hammering, crushing, intellectual machinery, which to all appearance works under such complete control, is set in movement by an enkindled, glowing imagination; and at the very centre of everything there is a panting, sobbing heart. Byron's faith helped him as much as did his scepticism. With perfect simplicity he takes the Old Testament story as he finds it. He treats its characters, not as symbolic figures, but as realities; and he does it in all sincerity— his scepticism attacks traditions; it accepts tradition. Besides, was he not himself, both in his intellect and his emotions, a man of the Old Testament type? In his soul resounded lamentations like those of Job when he was comforted and reproved by his friends, and cries for vengeance like those in the Psalms. The *Hebrew Melodies* prove how naturally the Jewish garment accommodated itself to the forms of his feeling.

In all sincerity, then, Byron for the time being acknowledges the claims of tradition and bows the neck of his reason to its yoke; but in *Cain* we see human reason writhing under this yoke, rebelling against it—tortured by its pricks and kicking against them. And what lends special attraction to the spectacle is, that the human reason in this case is a young, newborn one. On the true poet the rising of the sun makes as powerful an impression as if he were beholding it rise on the first day of creation; to Byron, all doubts and questions were so fresh that they could be put into the mouth of the first questioner and doubter. The formation of the doubts and complaints had demanded nothing less than the whole long succession of the human generations who had sighed and groaned over the cruelty of life and the irrationality of tradition. But although they are the accumulated woes of many thousand years—the ever increasing sufferings of thousands of generations of free human spirits in the torture-chambers of orthodoxy—which are here voiced by the first rebel, he expresses it all with as much originality and simplicity as if the thought-task of millions had at once been accomplished by the first thinking brain. This is the first of those contradictions in the poem which are so effective.

The part of the drama in which all the discrepancies in the Jewish-Christian tradition are laid bare, and its incompatibility as a whole with reason is proved—the veiled attack on orthodoxy, in short—possesses tolerably little interest for us nowadays; the human race has progressed so far since 1821 that all the subtlety displayed in refuting the theology of the Book of Genesis affects us much in the same manner as a disputation on the belief in werewolves. Nor are these attacks intended to be taken literally; Byron had, of course, no intention of writing blasphemously, of scoffing at a being whom he himself regarded as the supreme, the all-embracing being. What Cain combats is in reality only the belief that the order of nature is a moral order and that goodness, instead of being one of the aims of human life, is its postulate. It must be remembered that the language of human beings is full of words which were formed in ages past, and which we are obliged to use because the language owns no others, but the interpretation of which has changed many times in the course of centuries. Such words are, for example, soul and body, eternity, salvation, Paradise, the first temptation, the first curse. Byron has retained in his poem all the expressions of the Book of Genesis. The second suggestive contradiction in the drama is, therefore, the constant inward disagreement between the spirit of the poem and its letter. This second contradiction thoroughly arouses the readers who have been startled by the first.

Side by side in this drama with the exposure of the hollowness of the general orthodox belief in God, we have a passionate representation of the infinite misery of human existence. To what underlies this, the empty, unmeaning name of *pessimism* has been given; the true definition is, a profound compassion for the undeniable sufferings of humanity. Far deeper down in Byron's soul than wrath with the power which creates only to destroy, lies the feeling of the obligatory sympathy of all with all—sympathy with all the suffering which it is impossible to relieve, but equally impossible not to be conscious of. *Cain* is a tragedy dealing with the

source of all tragedy—the fact that man is born, suffers, sins, and dies.

Byron revolves in his mind the Bible legend: Adam has been tamed; Eve has been cowed; Abel is a gentle, submissive boy; Cain is young humanity—pondering, questioning, desiring, demanding. He is to take part in the general thanksgiving. Praise and give thanks for what? For life? Am I not to die? For life? Did I ask to live? Am I still in the garden of Eden? Why should I suffer? For Adam's transgression?

What had *I* done in this?—I was unborn:
I sought not to be born; nor love the state
To which that birth has brought me. Why did he
Yield to the serpent and the woman? Or,
Yielding, why suffer? What was there in this?
The tree was planted, and why not for him?
If not, why place him near it, where it grew,
The fairest in the centre? They have but
One answer to all questions: 'Twas *his* will,
And *he* is good.' How know I that? Because
He is all-powerful, must all-good, too, follow?

Goodness would not create evil, and what hath He created but evil? And even supposing evil leads to good?—why not create good at once? He has "multiplied himself in misery," and yet He is happy. Who could be happy alone, happy in being the only happy one? And that is what He is—the "indefinite, indissoluble tyrant."

We are nothing in His sight. "Well," says Cain, "if I am nothing, for nothing shall I be an hypocrite, and seem well-pleased with pain?" War of all with all, and death for all, and disease for nearly all, and suffering, and bitterness; these were the fruits of the forbidden tree. Is not man's lot a miserable one? One good gift the fatal apple has given—reason. But who could be proud of a mind which is chained to an enslaving body, "to the most gross and petty paltry wants, all foul and fulsome, the very best of its enjoyments a sweet degradation, a most enervating and filthy cheat!" Not Paradise, but death, is our inheritance on this wretched little earth, the abode of beings "whose enjoyment was to be in blindness—a Paradise of Ignorance, from which knowledge was barred as poison." And oh! the thought that all this misery is to be propagated and inherited!—to see the first tears shed and shudderingly anticipate the oceans that will flow! Would it not be better to snatch the infant in his sleep and dash him against the rocks, and thus choke the spring of misery at its source? Were it not infinitely better that the child had never been born? How dare any one bring children into such a world? And this is the existence for which I am to offer thanks and praise!

Such is Cain's mood at the moment when he is compelled to offer sacrifice; and it is largely due to the suggestions of Lucifer. For Lucifer prefers torment to "the smooth agonies of adulation, in hymns and harpings, and self-seeking prayers." This Lucifer is no devil. He says himself:

Who covets evil
For its own bitter sake?—*None*—nothing! 'tis
The leaven of all life, and lifelessness.

Nor is he a Mephistopheles. Except for one faint jest, he is severely earnest. No! this Lucifer is really the bringer of light, the genius of science, the proud and defiant spirit of criticism, the best friend of man, overthrown because he would not cringe or lie, but inflexible, because, like his enemy, he is eternal. He is the spirit of freedom. But it is significant that what he represents is not the frank, open, struggle for liberty, but the feeling which inspires gloomy conspirators, who seek their aim by forbidden ways—the feeling which prevailed among the despairing young friends of liberty in Europe in the year 1821.

In his work, *Justice in the Revolution and the Church*, Proudhon, addressing the Archbishop of Besançon, exclaims:

Liberty is your Antichrist. Come, then, O Satan! thou maligned of priests and kings, let me embrace thee, let me clasp thee to my heart! Thy works, thou blessed one, are not always fair and good, but they alone give meaning to the universe. What would justice be without thee? An instinct. Reason? A habit. Man? An animal.

Satan, thus understood, is simply the spirit of free criticism; and if Byron's poetry had been named "Satanic" after him, it might have borne the name without shame.

With the assistance of Lucifer, part of the action of *Cain* takes place in the region of the supernatural; for that spirit conveys his pupil through the abyss of space, shows him all the worlds with their inhabitants, the realms of death, and, through the mist of the future, the generations

yet unborn. He demands from Cain neither blind faith nor blind submission. He does not say: "Believe—and sink not! Doubt—and perish!" He does not make belief in him the condition of Cain's salvation; he requires neither homage nor gratitude; he opens Cain's eyes.

Cain returns to earth; and the first rebel leaves the first murderer alone, a prey to his consuming doubt. Sacrifices are to be offered, and he has to choose an altar. What are altars to him? So much turf and stone. Abhorring suffering, he will not slaughter innocent animals in honour of a bloodthirsty God; on his altar he lays the fruits of the earth.[15] Abel prays in correctly pious fashion. Cain, too, must pray. What shall he say?

If thou must be induced with altars
And softened with a sacrifice, receive them!
.   .   .   .   .   .
If thou lov'st blood, the shepherd's shrine,
  which smokes
On my right hand, hath shed it for thy service;
.   .   .   If a shrine without victim,
An altar without gore, may win thy favour,
Look on it! and for him who dresseth it,
He is—such as thou mad'st him; and seeks nothing
Which must be won by kneeling.

Fire comes down from heaven and consumes Abel's sacrifice, the flames greedily licking up the blood on the altar. But a whirlwind throws down Cain's altar and scatters the fruits upon the earth. Did God, then, rejoice in the pain of the bleating mothers when their lambs were taken from them to be slaughtered? and in "the pangs of the sad ignorant victims under the pious knife"? Cain's blood boils; he begins to demolish the offending altar. Abel opposes him. "Beware!" cries Cain; "thy God loves blood!" And, driven by his wrath, his misery, his fate, into the snare spread for him by the Lord, he commits the first murder, without knowing what it means to kill, and thus himself brings death to his kind—death, the very name of which, when the future of humanity was revealed to him, had filled him with horror. The deed is repented of before it is done; for Cain, who loves all men, is tenderly attached to Abel. There follow, nevertheless, the curse, the sentence, the banishment, and the mark of Cain.

---

[15] Here the influence of Shelley is apparent.

This mark of Cain is the mark of humanity—the sign of suffering and immortality. Byron's drama represents the struggle between suffering, searching, striving humanity and that God of hosts, of lightnings, and of storms, whose weakened arms are forced to let go a world which is writhing itself free from his embrace. To exterminate this world which denies him, he causes rivers of blood to flow, and hundreds of martyr fires to be kindled by his priests; but Cain rises unscathed from the ashes of the fire, and flagellates the priests with undying scorn. Cain is thinking humanity, which with its thought cleaves the old "firmament of heaven," and beholds millions of spheres rolling in freedom, high above Jehovah's rattling thunder-chariot. Cain is working humanity, which is striving in the sweat of its brow to produce a new and better Eden—not the Eden of ignorance, but an Eden of knowledge and harmony; a humanity which, long after Jehovah has been sewn into His shroud, will be alive, pressing to its breast Abel, who has been restored from the dead.[16]

Cain was dedicated to Sir Walter Scott, who gave it as his opinion that Byron's Muse had never before taken so lofty a flight, and who answered in advance the attacks that were likely to be made on the author. But this did not prevent the appearance of the work being regarded and lamented as a positive national calamity. Before it went to press, Murray was anxious that Byron should make some alterations. But Byron wrote:

The two passages cannot be altered without making Lucifer talk like the Bishop of Lincoln, which would not be in the character of the former."

Immediately after publication the play was pirated, and Murray applied to Lord Eldon for an injunction to protect his property in the work. The Lord Chancellor refused it in terms which may be epitomised thus: "This court, like the other courts of justice in this country, acknowledges Christianity as part of the law of the land. Its jurisdiction in protecting literary property is founded on this. The publication in question being intended to bring into discredit that portion of Scripture history to which it relates, no damages can be recovered in respect of a piracy of it." Thus *Cain*—like Southey's *Wat Tyler*—was regarded as such a criminal work that the law refused even to vindicate the right of property in it.

Meanwhile, Moore was writing to Byron:

Cain is wonderful, terrible, never to be forgotten. If I am not mistaken, it will sink deep into the world's heart."

History has endorsed this verdict.

[16] Compare Leconte de Lisle: *Poèmes barbares. Kain.*

XXI

COMIC AND TRAGIC REALISM

WHEN, IN THE AUTUMN OF 1816, Switzerland began to be overrun by crowds of English tourists, residence there became intolerable to Lord Byron, and he betook himself with Mr. Hobhouse, the travelling companion of his youth, to Italy. At Milan he met Beyle, one of the most acute of observers; and it is a strong proof of the extraordinary impression produced by the poet's personality, that he captivated even this man, who was always on his guard against being led into hasty enthusiasms, and who quickly detected what was assumed in Byron's manner. Beyle writes:

"Ce fut pendant l'automne de 1816, que je le rencontrai au théâtre de la *Scala*, à Milan, dans la loge de M. Louis de Brême. Je fus frappé des yeux de Lord Byron au moment où il écoutait un sestetto d'un opéra de Mayer intitulé *Elena*. Je n'ai vu de ma vie rien de plus beau ni de plus expressif. Encore aujourd'hui, si je viens à penser à l'expression qu'un grand peintre devrait donner au génie, cette tête sublime reparaît tout-à-coup devant moi. J'eus un instant d'enthousiasme … Je n'oublierai jamais l'expression divine de ses traits; c'était l'air serein de la puissance et du génie."

From Milan Byron proceeded to Venice, the city which he preferred to all others, and which he has celebrated in the Fourth Canto of *Childe Harold*, in *Marino Faliero*, in *The Two Foscari*, in the *Ode to Venice*, and in *Beppo*, which last work was written in Venice. Never had he been overcome by such deep depression as now; never had forgetfulness been so desirable. The enchanting climate and air of Italy acted on him like a charm. He was twenty-nine. With its beautiful women, its loose morals, and all its southern manners and customs, Venice invited to a wild revel of the senses. An ardent

longing for happiness and enjoyment was part of Byron's nature; and it is also to be remembered that his defiant temper had been thoroughly roused. He had been stigmatised as capable of every enormity; he might just as well, for once, give his countrymen abroad something real to write home about, and the old women at home real cause to swoon; they wrote and they swooned whatever his behaviour was.

His first proceedings in Venice were to engage a gondola and gondolier, a box at the theatre, and a mistress. The last was easily found. He had taken apartments in the house of a merchant, whose wife, Marianna Segati, then aged twenty-two, he describes as having large, black, Oriental eyes and being in "appearance altogether like an antelope." She and Byron became so enamoured of each other, that Byron allowed Hobhouse to go on alone to Rome. "I should have gone too," he writes, "but I fell in love, and must stay that over." The young beauty compelled him to join, in her company, in all the distractions of the Carnival. He devoted his nights, like the born Venetian, to pleasure; but in his fear of becoming stout, he adhered to his usual extremely sparing diet, ate only vegetables and fruit, and was obliged to drink large quantities of his favourite beverage, rum and water, to keep up his strength. For he was completing *Manfred* at this time. We receive a sad impression of the aimlessness of his life when we read that, to counterbalance all the distractions, to give his days a centre of gravity, he spent several hours of each at the Armenian monastery of San Lazaro, learning Armenian from the monks. The mornings were devoted to this, the afternoons to physical exercise, chiefly riding. He had his horses brought to Venice, and with Shelley and other friends used to cross over to the Lido and ride there.

We have a reminiscence of the talk during these rides in Shelley's *Julian and Maddalo*. At sunset he and Byron see on one of the islands a dreary, windowless pile, rising in dark relief against the flaming sky behind it. They hear, clanging from the open tower on the top of the house, the iron tongue of a bell. Said Byron:—

> What we behold
> Shall be the madhouse and its belfry tower,
> .   .   .   and ever at this hour
> Those who may cross the water, hear that bell
> Which calls the maniacs, each one from his cell
> To vespers .   .   .   .
> And like that black and dreary bell, the soul
> Hung in a heaven-illumined tower, must toll
> Our thoughts and our desires to meet below
> Round the rent heart and pray—as madmen do
> For what—they know not.

No better image of Byron's own life at this period could be desired. Most assuredly at this time his longings and desires were like maniacs, all gathered together only once a day by the bell of the madhouse.

It was with difficulty, after being ill with a sharp fever, contracted in the unhealthy air of Venice, that he tore himself away from Marianna Segati long enough to pay a short visit to Ferrara and Rome. After his return, however, his violent passion for her subsided, as he began to discover that she sold the jewellery he gave her, and made as much profit generally as she could, out of her position as his mistress. During the first part of his stay in Venice, Byron had mixed much in the refined society which had its chief meeting-place at the house of the cultivated, literary Countess Albrizzi; now he withdrew himself entirely from its restraining influence. He rented for himself and his menagerie a magnificent palace on the Grand Canal. This palace soon became a harem, in which the favourite sultana was a beautiful young woman of the lower orders, Margarita Cogni, who, from the circumstance of her husband being a baker, was called Byron's Fornarina. Her face was of "the fine Venetian cast of the old time"; her figure, though she was perhaps rather tall, was also fine, and exactly suited the national dress. She had all the naïveté and droll humour of the Venetian lower classes, and, as she could neither read nor write, she could not plague Byron with letters. She was jealous; she snatched off the masks of ladies whom she found in Byron's company, and she sought his presence whenever it suited her, with no great regard to time, place, or persons. He writes:

When I first knew her, I was in 'relazione' with la Signora, who was silly enough one evening at Dolo, accompanied by some of her female friends, to threaten her … Margarita threw back her veil (fazziolo), and replied in very explicit Venetian, 'You are *not* his *wife*. I am *not* his *wife*: you are his Donna, and *I* am his *Donna*: your husband is a *becco*, and mine is another. For the rest, what *right* have you to reproach me? If he prefers me to you, is it my fault?' Having delivered this pretty piece of eloquence, she went on her way, leaving a numerous audience with Madame—to ponder at her leisure on the dialogue between them.

In time Margarita established herself as housekeeper in Byron's house, reduced the expenses of the establishment to less than half, marched about in a gown with a train, and wore a hat with feathers (articles of dress which had been the height of her ambition), beat the maids, opened Byron's letters, and actually studied her alphabet in order to be able to detect which of them were from ladies. In her wild way she loved him; her joy at seeing him return safe from a sail in which his boat had been caught in a storm, was that of a tigress over her returned cubs. Her ungovernableness increased to such an extent that Byron was obliged to tell her that she must return home. After trying to attack him with a knife, she threw herself in her anger and despair into the canal. She was rescued and sent home, and Byron wrote her story at full length to Murray; he knew that his letters to his publisher were passed from hand to hand like public documents; and half the pleasure of his excesses consisted in the certainty of their creating a scandal in England.

From the letter just quoted it is easy to see that the dissolute Venetian life did not absorb him heart and soul; he quite saw the comic side of it all. And it was actually of service in furthering his development as a thinker and a poet. His friends at home were in despair at the way in which he was compromising his dignity and his reputation; but this wild, jovial, Carnival life, lived amongst the women of the people under the bright Italian skies, was producing a new, realistic style in his poetry. In the works of his youth he had, sadly, and with a heart wrung with anguish, described the ebb-tide of life; in *Beppo* the spring-tide suddenly began to rise. *Beppo* was real life, in a setting of laughter and jest. In Byron's youthful pathos there had been a certain monotony, along with a good deal of artificiality. In this work his genius, as it were, sloughed its skin; the monotony was broken by a constant change of theme and key, the artificiality was dispelled by hearty laughter. In his youthful satire there had been a good deal of snappishness and a decided lack of grace and humour. Now that his own life had for a short time assumed the character of a Carnival play, the Graces, of their own accord, came tripping and twining through his verses, keeping time to the tinkling of the bells of humour.

Beppo is the "Carnival of Venice" itself—that old theme which Byron, like another Paganini, found upon his way, lifted on the point of his divine bow, and proceeded to adorn with a multitude of daring and ingenious variations, with a luxurious embroidery of pearls and golden arabesques. There had come into his hands an English comic poem on the subject of King Arthur and the Knights of the Round Table, in which the Honourable John Hookham Frere had imitated the first poem written in the *ottava rima* (Berni's paraphrase of *Orlando Furioso*). The reading of Frere's work aroused in Byron the desire to attempt something in the same style, and the result was *Beppo*, the complete originality of which effaced every recollection of a model. Now he had found the form which suited his purpose, the weapon which he could wield with the most effect—the *ottava rima*, with its sextett of alternate rhymes, to the solid mass of which the concluding rhymed couplet adds now a jest, now a key, now a stylistic antic, now a stinging wit-dart.

And what is the poem about? About just as little as Alfred de Musset's *Namouna*, or Paludan-Müller's *Danserinden*, which were written in much the same style sixteen years later (1833). The story in itself is nothing: A Venetian goes to sea, and stays so long away that his wife makes sure he is dead. She has long been as good as married to another man, when he suddenly turns up again. He has been sold as a Turkish slave, and, on his return, dressed as a Turk, he finds his wife at a masked ball, on the arm of the Count who has now for several years filled his place. When the couple, returning from the ball, step out of their gondola, they find the husband standing at the door of his own house. As soon as all three have recovered a little from the first surprise, they call for three cups of coffee, and conversation begins in the following style, Laura speaking:

Beppo! what's your pagan name?
Bless me! your beard is of amazing growth!
And how came you to keep away so long?
Are you not sensible 'twas very wrong?

And are you *really, truly*, now a Turk?
With any other women did you wive?
Is't true they use their fingers for a fork?
Well, that's the prettiest shawl!—as I'm alive!
You'll give it me! They say you eat no pork,

This is all the explanation the husband receives, or asks. As he cannot go about dressed as a Turk, he borrows a pair of trousers from Laura's *cavaliere servente*, the Count, and the story ends in perfect amicability on all sides. In itself it is of little importance, but it was Byron's study for his masterpiece, *Don Juan*—the only one of his works which, as it were, contains the whole wide ocean of life, with its storms and its sunshine, its ebb and its flood.

Byron's friends tried every means in their power to induce him to return to England, in the hope of thereby reclaiming him from the life he was leading. But instead of returning he sold Newstead Abbey, which in his youth he had vowed he would never part with (receiving £94,000 for it). Indeed, so strong was his antipathy to the thought of return, that he could not even bear the idea of being taken back as a corpse. He writes:

I trust they won't think of 'pickling, and bringing me home to Clod or Blunderbuss Hall.' I am sure my bones would not rest in an English grave, or my clay mix with the earth of that country. I believe the thought would drive me mad on my deathbed, could I suppose that any of my friends would be base enough to convey my carcass back to your soil. I would not even feed your worms, if I could help it.

But now occurred an event which in an unforeseen manner put an end to the polygamy in which Byron was living in Venice—an event that constituted a turning-point in his life. In April 1819, he was presented to Countess Teresa Guiccioli, daughter of Count Gamba of Ravenna, a lady who was at this time only sixteen, and had just been married to Count Guiccioli, a man of sixty, who had been twice left a widower.

The introduction took place against the inclination of both; the young Countess was tired that evening and longed to go home, and Byron was unwilling to make new acquaintances; both assented only from the desire to oblige their hostess. But no sooner had they entered into conversation than a spark, which was never extinguished, passed from soul to soul. The Countess afterwards wrote:—

His noble and exquisitely beautiful countenance, the tone of his voice, his manners, the thousand enchantments that surrounded him, rendered him so different and so superior a being to any whom I had hitherto seen, that it was impossible he should not have left the most profound impression upon me. From that evening, during the whole of my subsequent stay at Venice, we met every day.

A few weeks later, Teresa was obliged to return with her husband to Ravenna. The parting with Byron agitated her so terribly that during the course of the first day's journey she fainted several times; and she became so ill that she arrived at Ravenna half dead. She was also much distressed at this time by the loss of her mother. The Count owned several houses on the road from Venice to Ravenna, and it was his habit to stop at these mansions, one after the other, on his journeys between the two cities. From each the enamoured young Countess now wrote to Byron, expressing in the most passionate and pathetic terms her despair at leaving him, and entreating him to come to Ravenna. Very touching is the description which she gives, after her arrival, of the complete change in all her feelings. She, who formerly had thought of nothing but balls and fêtes, has, she says, been so entirely changed by her love that solitude has become dear and welcome to her. She will, according to Byron's wish, "avoid all general society, and devote herself to reading, music, domestic occupations, riding"—everything, in short, that she knew he would most like. Longing and grief brought on a dangerous fever, and symptoms of consumption showed themselves. Then Byron set out for Ravenna. He found the Countess in bed, apparently in a very serious condition. He writes:

I greatly fear that she is going into a consumption … Thus it is with every thing and every body for whom I feel anything like a real attachment … If anything happens to my present Amica, I have done with the passion for ever—it is my last love. As to libertinism, I have sickened myself of that, as was natural in the way I went on, and I have at least derived that advantage from vice, to *love* in the better sense of the word.

The attitude assumed towards the young foreigner by the Count astonished every one; he showed him all manner of polite attentions; used to come for him every day with a "coach and six," and drive about the country with him, like "Whittington with his cat," Byron declared.

It was a happy time for Byron. This, his one perfect and fully returned attachment, brought back all the emotions of his youth. The beautiful *Stanzas to the Po*, which reveal deep, chivalrous feeling, and end with the prayer, "Let me perish young!" were the first-fruits of the new passion. He loved truly and with his whole heart, and loved like a youth, without at any point taking up a position outside of his feeling or attempting to rise superior to it. When, in August, the Countess was obliged to accompany her husband on his visits to his other estate, Byron went daily to her house, and, causing her apartments to be opened, sat turning over her books and writing in them. On the last page of a copy of *Corinne* he wrote the following note:—

MY DEAREST TERESA—I have read this book in your garden;—my love, you were absent, or else I could not have read it. It is a favourite book of yours, and the writer was a friend of mine. You will not understand these English words, and *others* will not understand them—which is the reason I have not scrawled them in Italian. But you will recognise the handwriting of him who so passionately loved you, and you will divine that, over a book which was yours, he could only think of love. In that word, beautiful in all languages, but most so in yours—*Amor mio*—is comprised my existence here and hereafter … Think of me, some times, when the Alps and the ocean divide us—but they never will, unless you *wish* it.   BYRON.
BOLOGNA, *August* 25, 1819.

It is needless to compare the expressions in this note with those of the farewell letter to Lady Caroline Lamb; one feels at once that this is the language of a truer love.

When, in September, Count Guiccioli was called away by business to Ravenna, he left the young Countess and her lover to the free enjoyment of each other's society at Bologna; and he was quite agreeable, when the physicians ordered her to Venice, that Lord Byron should be the companion of her journey. Byron had a villa at La Mira, near Venice; he placed it at her disposal, and resided there with her. Of the journey and the ensuing period she wrote to Moore after Byron's death:

But I cannot linger over these recollections of happiness;—the contrast with the present is too dreadful. If a blessed spirit, while in the full enjoyment of heavenly happiness, were sent down to this earth to suffer all its miseries, the contrast could not be more dreadful between the past and the present, than what I have endured from the moment when that terrible word reached my ears, and I for ever lost the hope of again beholding him, one look from whom I valued beyond all earth's happiness.

The woman to whom the world owes a debt of gratitude for having saved Byron from ruining himself by degrading dissipation, lost her standing in the eyes of Italian society from the moment when she took up her residence in her lover's house. The Italian moral code of that day—of which De Stendhal's Italian tales give an excellent idea— permitted a young married woman to have a friend (*Amico*); and, indeed, regarded him practically as her husband, but only on the condition that those outward conventions were respected, which Countess Guiccioli was now disregarding.

It was not light-mindedness that led her to expose herself to the censure of public opinion. She saw her own relation to Lord Byron in a poetic light; she regarded it as her mission to free a noble and gifted poet from the fetters of ignoble connections, and to restore his faith in pure and self-sacrificing love. She hoped to act on him as a Muse. She was very young, and very beautiful—fair, with dark eyes; small, but beautifully proportioned. West, the American painter, to whom Byron sat for his portrait at the Villa Rossa, near Pisa, gives the following description of her:—

Whilst I was painting, the window from which I received my light became suddenly darkened, and I heard a voice exclaim: '*E troppo bello!*' I turned, and discovered a beautiful female stooping down to look in, the ground on the outside being on a level with the bottom of the window. Her long golden hair hung down about her face and shoulders, her complexion was exquisite, and her smile completed one of the most romantic-looking heads, set off as it was by the bright sun behind it, which I had ever beheld.

The more important it became to the Countess not to be regarded simply as one of Byron's many mistresses, the more did she endeavour to raise his poetry into a higher and purer atmosphere than that in which it moved at this time.

One evening when he was sitting turning over the leaves of the manuscript of *Don Juan*, two cantos of which had been completed before his acquaintance with the Countess began, she leant over his shoulder, pointed to a verse on the page he was just turning, and asked him what it meant. Byron writes:

She had stumbled by mere chance on the 137th stanza of the First Canto. I told her 'Nothing; but your husband is coming.' As I said this in Italian with some emphasis, she started up in a fright, and said, 'Oh, my God, is he coming?' thinking it was her own.

But this accident aroused her curiosity regarding *Don Juan*; she read the two cantos in a French translation; her delicacy was shocked by the indecency of much of the contents, and she implored Byron not to go on with the poem. He at once promised what his *Dictatrice* demanded. This was Countess Guiccioli's first direct influence upon Byron's work—and it was certainly not a beneficial one; but she soon withdrew her prohibition, on the condition, however, that there should be no obscenity in the part as yet unwritten. A whole series of fine works which now proceeded from Byron's pen are the beautiful and enduring mementos of his life with her. The manner in which in *Don Juan* he tore the veil from all illusions, and mercilessly mocked at sentimentality, wounded the Countess's womanly feelings; for woman is ever unwilling that the illusions which, as long as they last, beautify life, should be rudely dispelled.

Countess Guiccioli, thus, did her utmost to prevent Byron writing works calculated to destroy belief in human nature and the value of life. The themes which she, the romantic lover of the grand, and the ardent Italian patriot, led him to choose, were themes calculated to elevate her countrymen's minds and quicken their desire for the emancipation of their country from a foreign yoke. It was to gratify her that he wrote *The Prophecy of Dante*, and translated from the *Inferno* the famous episode of *Francesca of Rimini*; and it was under her influence that he wrote the Venetian dramas, *Marino Faliero* and *The Two Foscari*, plays which, though they are written in English, really belong, from their style and subject, rather to Romance than to English literature—just as they belong, as a matter of fact, to the Italian, not the English, stage. They are plays with a passionate political purpose, written in careless, and occasionally ill-sounding iambics. Their aim was, by the employment of the strongest means possible, to excite the lethargic Italian patriots to unanimous revolt against the oppressors. They are scenically effective. Whilst under the first impression of his attachment to the Countess, Byron also wrote *Mazeppa*, the heroine of which bears her name; and her personality was directly transferred to the two best and most beautiful female characters which he created at this period—Adah in *Cain*, and Myrrha in *Sardanapalus*.

In Countess Guiccioli Byron found the realisation of the ideal of femininity which had always been before his eyes, but which in his earlier narrative poems he had not succeeded in portraying naturally. He himself naively confessed to Lady Blessington the difficulty in which he found himself, and the manner in which he personified his ideals. He said:

I detest thin women, and unfortunately all, or nearly all plump women have clumsy hands and feet, so that I am obliged to have recourse to imagination for my beauties, and there I always find them. I flatter myself that my Leila, Zuleika, Gulnare, Medora, and Haidée will always vouch for my taste in beauty; these are the bright creations of my fancy, with rounded forms, and delicacy of limbs, nearly so incompatible as to be rarely, if ever, united … You must have observed that I give my heroines extreme refinement, joined to great simplicity and want of education. Now, refinement and want of education are incompatible, at least, I have ever found them so: so here again, you see, I am forced to have recourse to imagination.

The concoctions were as impossible as they were beautiful; these fair ones produced next to no impression of reality, herein resembling the heroes whom they worshipped.

From *The Giaour* to *The Siege of Corinth*, Byron's narrative poems are of the Romantic type, but bear the imprint of a strong individuality. Passion is idolised in both sexes. The heroes are, to borrow an expression from *The Giaour*, "wracks, by passion left behind"; but "wracks" which choose rather to continue being tossed by its tempests than to live in drowsy tranquillity. They do not love with the cold love begotten of a cold climate; theirs "is like a lava flood." The most characteristic of these now extremely antiquated Byronic heroes is the noble Corsair—who is proud, capricious, scornful, revengeful to the point of cruelty, a prey to remorse, and so nobly magnanimous that he will rather submit to the most barbarous tortures than kill a sleeping enemy. This interesting bandit, with his mysterious countenance, his theatrical deportment, and his boundless chivalry towards woman, is the Byronic counterpart of Schiller's Karl Moor. The sovereign of a law-abiding people, hampered by the conventions of a court, could not be Byron's ideal man; there was no possibility in such a life of romantic exploits, of perils by land or by water. So he took a pirate chieftain, and, to the qualities induced by such a man's manner of life, superadded the finest qualities of his own soul. The Corsair, who is accustomed to wade in blood, turns with a shudder from the young Sultana who loves him, when he sees the little spot of blood on her forehead—not because it is imaginable that a Conrad would have shuddered at so little, but because Byron himself would have shrunk from such a sight. It has been cleverly said that the real reason of the marvellous attraction of all the heroes and heroines of these poems of Byron's youth for the general public was, that they all moved where they had no joints. The public were not more enraptured by the passion of the lyric portions and by the poetical gems inserted here and there (almost always during the process of proof-reading), than by the deeds which were really impossible to human nature. It was admiration of the same kind as is displayed for the daring acrobat, who does breakneck feats by unnatural contortions of his body.

But in these same characters some of the finer, deeper-lying qualities of Byron's ideal also revealed themselves. Conrad's inflexibility under suffering foreshadows Manfred's; and he will no more bow the knee than will Cain to Lucifer, or Don Juan to Gulbeyaz. Compassion for those less fortunately situated than himself, a feeling which never disappeared from Byron's soul, exists, though chiefly in the shape of hatred of despots, in Lara; and in both *The Giaour* and *The Siege of Corinth* we have the longing for the emancipation of Greece.

It was a strange ordering of destiny that the poet himself should end his life as a commander of just such wild men as those he had described. The Viking blood in his veins gave him no rest until he himself became a Viking leader, like the Normans from whom he was descended. And even if all these desperadoes (Alp, the renegade, who leads the Turks against his countrymen, no less than Lara, who makes war on his peers) are simply the imaginary creatures of the poet's brain, there is in the characters of all, one realistic trait, a trait which also develops in those who attach themselves to them—the proud endurance of terrible fates. The humour of *Beppo* is the form in which naturalness overcomes the staginess and artificiality of Byron's earlier works. The sympathy with human suffering, which in his serious poetry gradually swallows up all other sympathies, is the form in which the feeling of the reality of life prevails over his Romanticism and supersedes it.

This feeling gained in intensity after his breach with England. *The Prisoner of Chillon* had described the suffering of the noble Bonnivard, who for six long years was chained to a pillar in an underground dungeon by a chain too short to allow of his lying down, and compelled to witness the agonies and death of his brothers, who were fettered in the same manner, without being able to put out his hand to help them. On it followed *Mazeppa*—the youth bound to the back of the wild horse, which gallops with dripping mane and steaming flanks through the forests and across the steppes, whilst he, torn from the arms of his beloved, whose fate is unknown to him, and looking forward to a horrible fate himself, suffers agonies of thirst, pain, and shame. So far Byron has by preference dwelt upon the things that are most terrible to flesh and blood; even when, as in the case of Bonnivard, there was a spiritual element in the suffering, and the theme presented an opportunity for the description of a heroic personality, he dwelt most on the purely physical torture. But now that

his sympathies were aroused for the great martyrs of Italy, his conception of the tragic was ennobled.

In *The Prophecy of Dante* he thus describes the lot of the poet:—

Many are poets, but without the name,
    For what is poesy but to create
    From overfeeling good or ill; and aim
At an external life beyond our fate,
    And be the new Prometheus of new men,
    Bestowing fire from heaven, and then, too late,
Finding the pleasure given repaid with pain,
    And vultures to the heart of the bestower,
    Who, having lavish'd his high gift in vain,
Lies chain'd to his lone rock by the sea-shore.

And he makes the great poet, who was, like himself, unjustly exiled, exclaim;

                'Tis the doom
    Of spirits of my order to be rack'd
In life, to wear their hearts out, and consume
    Their days in endless strife, and die alone.

Of Tasso Byron had already written. Even a superficial comparison of Goethe's *Tasso* with Byron's *Lament of Tasso* is sufficient to show us what a resistless attraction hopeless suffering had for Byron's imagination. Goethe takes Tasso the youth, the lover, the poet, and places him in the society of the beautiful women of the court of Ferrara, where, happy and unhappy, he is admired and humiliated. Byron takes Tasso alone, ruined, shut out from society, shut into the cell of a madhouse though he is quite sane, a prey to the cruelty of his former protectors:—

I loved all solitude—but little thought
To spend I know not what of life, remote
From all communion with existence, save
The maniac and his tyrant;—had I been
Their fellow, many years ere this had seen
My mind like theirs corrupted to its grave.
But who hath seen me writhe, or heard me rave?
Perchance in such a cell we suffer more
Than the wreck'd sailor on his desert shore;
The world is all before him—*mine* is *here*,
Scarce twice the space they must accord my bier.
What though *he* perish, he may lift his eye,
And with a dying glance upbraid the sky;
I will not raise my own in such reproof,
Although 'tis clouded by my dungeon roof.

Of the court of Ferrara, a court where Lucrezia Borgia has her residence, a court where the passions and the cruelty of the Renaissance period flourish, Goethe makes a little German Weimar, where everything is ruled by the most refined humanitarianism of the eighteenth century; Byron is magnetically attracted by what he considers the revolting barbarity of the Duke of Ferrara, and his poem turns into a declamation against the injustice and tyranny of princes.

We have another description of tragic suffering, along with still more violent accusation—both, however, decidedly overdone—in *The Two Foscari*, a tragedy in which a father is compelled to sentence the son he loves to the agonies of the torture-chamber, and in which the son, who is the hero of the tragedy, is stretched on the rack during almost the whole duration of the play, and only rises from it to die of grief because he is banished. In *The Two Foscari*, as in his other tragedies, Byron, as if in defiance, follows the French fashion of strict adherence to the Aristotelian rules. In his conviction that this is the one right style, he risks the comical paradox, that England has hitherto possessed no drama.

It has created much surprise that Byron, who, like all the other English poets of the day, was a pronounced Naturalist—which means that he preferred the forest to the garden, the unsophisticated to the civilised human being, the original to the acquired language of passion—that this same Byron should have been such an enthusiastic admirer of Pope and of the small group of poets (including Samuel Rogers and Crabbe) who still paid homage to classical tradition, even to the extent of imitating the antique dramatic style.

The first reason for the admiration of Pope is to be sought in Byron's spirit of contradiction. The fact that the poets of that Lake School which he despised were continually reviling Pope, was in itself a sufficient reason for his exalting him to the skies, calling him the greatest of all English poets, and declaring that he would willingly himself defray the expense of erecting a monument to him in the Poet's Corner of Westminster Abbey, from which, as a Catholic, he was excluded. Secondly, we have to remember that the traditions of Harrow never lost their influence over Byron; and at Harrow Pope had always been held up as the model poet. A third thing to be remembered is Byron's own great deficiency in critical acumen, as an instance of which we may take his remark to Lady Blessington

that Shakespeare owed half his fame to his low birth. There still remain the predisposing circumstances—that Pope was deformed, and in spite of his deformity had a beautiful head; that he did not belong to the Established Church; that he was the poet of good society; and that his deformity begot in him a certain satirical gloom—all things in which Byron sympathised with him. And, lastly, we have Byron's personal bias (possibly attributable to his Norman descent) towards rhetoric of the style peculiar to the Latin races.

The circumstance that Byron championed the art theories of a past age, whilst he in everything else belonged to the party of progress, produces a certain likeness between him and Armand Carrel, who also remained faithful to antiquated classicism in literature, though he held the most emancipated views in politics and religion. As both of them adopted the standpoint of eighteenth century France in most matters intellectual and spiritual, it was not unnatural that they should also conform to it in the only domain in which it was a conventional standpoint, namely, that of *belles-lettres*. Certain it is that his theoretical caprices had a baneful influence on Byron's Italian dramas. These consist of monologues and declamation. Byron's genius and Countess Guiccioli's patriotism combined did not suffice to communicate to them more than a very meagre quantum of poetic inspiration.

But during the production of *Cain* and *Sardanapalus* the young Countess was what it was her desire to be, Byron's Muse.

The best thing in *Cain* is the character of Adah. It has been often remarked that Byron's male characters all resemble one another; what his critics have been less apt to observe is, how dissimilar his women are. Adah is not a female Cain, though she is the one imaginable wife for him. Cain's female counterpart is the proud, defiant Aholibamah of *Heaven and Earth*. Cain sees annihilation everywhere; Adah sees growth, love, germinating power, happiness. To Cain, the cypress which spreads its branches above little Enoch's head is a tree of mourning; all Adah sees is that it gives shade to the child. After Cain has despairingly made it plain to himself and Adah that all the world's evils and misfortunes are to be transmitted through Enoch, Adah says:

Oh, Cain, look on him; see how full of life,
Of strength, of bloom, of beauty, and of joy,
How like to me—how like to thee, when gentle!

Out of so little is Adah made, that all her speeches put together would not occupy one octavo page. When Cain has to make his choice between love and knowledge, she says: "Oh, Cain! choose love." When Cain, having killed Abel, stands alone, cursed and avoided as a murderer, she answers his ejaculation of: "Leave me!," with the words: "Why, all have left thee." And this character Byron created almost without departing from the letter of the Bible, simply by sometimes putting what is really said by one into the mouth of another. In Genesis, Cain, when he has been cursed by the Lord, says: "My punishment is greater than I can bear," &c. In Byron's play, Cain, when the terrible curse of the angel has fallen, stands mute; but Adah lifts up her voice and says:

> This punishment is more than he can bear.
> Behold, thou driest him from the face of earth,
> And from the face of God shall he be hid.
> A fugitive and vagabond on earth,
> 'Twill come to pass that whoso findeth him
> Shall slay him—

the exact words which the Bible puts into the mouth of Cain. Byron, with the eye of genius, saw in this one utterance, this Old Testament lump of clay, the outlines of a whole human figure; and with nothing but the pressure of his hand moulded it into a statuette of the first loving woman.

The other character in which we feel, and feel still more strongly, the influence of the young Countess, is Myrrha, the Greek female slave in *Sardanapalus*. *Sardanapalus* is the best of Byron's historical tragedies.—With careless contempt for his fellow-men and the world in general, the proud Sardanapalus has given himself up to voluptuous pleasures. Martial fame he despises; he cares not to win a great name by shedding the blood of thousands of unoffending human beings; and as little does he desire to be worshipped, like his fathers, as a god. His careless magnanimity amounts to imprudence. He returns to the rebel priest the sword which has been snatched from him, with the words:

> Receive your sword, and know
> That I prefer your service militant
> Unto your ministry—not loving either.

His manly vigour appears to be ebbing away in a life of voluptuous enjoyment, when Myrrha, the Ionian, his favourite slave, determines to rescue him. She implores him to rouse himself, and prepare to defend himself against his enemies. It is almost as great a grief to her that she loves him as that she is a slave.

> Why do I love this man? My country's daughters
> Love none but heroes. But I have no country!
> The slave has lost all save her bonds. I love him;
> And that's the heaviest link of the long chain—
> To love whom we esteem not … .. . .
> And yet methinks I love him more, perceiving
> That he is hated of his own barbarians.

But when the enemies attack the palace, and Sardanapalus, after rejecting the clumsy sword as hurting his hand, and the heavy helmet as "a mountain on his temples," plunges bareheaded and lightly armed into the midst of the fray and fights like a hero, Myrrha triumphs as if a burden of shame were lifted from her heart:—

> 'Tis no dishonour—no—
> 'Tis no dishonour to have loved this man.
> .   .   .   .   .   .
> .   .   .   .   . If Alcides
> Were shamed in wearing Lydian Omphale's
> She-garb, and wielding her vile distaff, surely
> He, who springs up a Hercules at once,
> Nursed in effeminate arts from youth to
>   manhood,
> And rushes from the banquet to the battle,
> As though it were a bed of love, deserves
> That a Greek girl should be his paramour,
> And a Greek bard his minstrel, a Greek tomb
> His monument."

It is as if Byron were prophesying his own fate. And was it not true of the poet, as of his hero, that he had known a thousand women, but never a true woman's heart till now?

> MYRRHA. Then thou wouldst know what thou
>   canst never know.
> SARDANAPALUS. And that is—
> MYRRHA. The true value of a heart;
>   At least, a woman's.
> SARDANAPALUS. I have proved a thousand—
>   A thousand, and a thousand.
> MYRRHA. Hearts?
> SARDANAPALUS. I think so.
> MYRRHA. Not one! The time may come thou may'st."

Like Myrrha, the young Italian Countess set before her lover more manly aims than voluptuous enjoyment; like Myrrha, she rescued him from a life which was unworthy of his great and noble mind.

We left the lovers at the country house of La Mira, near Venice, where Byron wrote, amongst other things, the Memoirs which he presented to Thomas Moore, to be left as a legacy to the latter's little son, but which were burned at the instigation of Byron's family, and for reasons which have never been satisfactorily explained. The peaceful life at La Mira was not of long duration. Count Guiccioli suddenly determined that he would put an end to the existing state of matters. The Countess would not give up Byron, and a separation from her husband was the result. With the consent of her family, she relinquished fortune and position in society; a small yearly allowance was to be paid her; but the conditions of the separation only held good as long as she continued to reside in her father's house. Here Byron regularly spent his evenings with her; he loved to hear her play, or sing airs by Mozart or Rossini. His diary of January and February 1821 chiefly consists of the following regularly repeated entries:

Rode—fired pistols—dined—wrote—visited —heard music—talked nonsense—went home—read.

As long as Count Guiccioli was still playing the rôle of possible avenger, the situation had contained the element of danger and excitement which to Byron was the spice of life. He believed that he owed his safety from assassination in the course of his rides to the fact of his being known to carry pistols and to have an unerring aim, and from assassination at home to the avaricious Count's disinclination to pay the twenty scudi which were the hire of a first-class bravo. This excitement was now at an end, but there was substituted for it a new and nobler one.

The whole Italian peninsula was in a state of silent but violent ferment. After the overthrow of Napoleon's rule, the old rulers "by the grace of God" had at once begun to conduct themselves with overweening arrogance. Every trace of French influence in the shape of beneficent reform was to be effaced, and the old abuses were to be re-introduced. The unbearable oppression during the general European reaction which followed the formation of the Holy Alliance, drove the Italians to

form a wide-spread conspiracy; great secret leagues of the Carbonari, imitated from those of the Freemasons, were soon in existence in all parts of the country.

The Countess introduced Byron into the circle of the conspirators. The whole Gamba family belonged to the secret society. The Countess's brother, Pietro, a warmhearted youth of twenty, who was an enthusiastic admirer of Byron and eventually accompanied him to Greece, was one of its most ardent and best-informed leaders. Carbonarism seemed to Byron the poetry of politics. The wooden Parliamentary politics of his native country had repelled him, but this appealed strongly to his imagination. He was advanced to a high rank in the society, and was made chief of a division called the Americani. He provided the conspirators with supplies of weapons, and offered the "constitutional" government at Naples one thousand Louis-d'ors as his contribution to the expenses of carrying on the war against the Holy Alliance. His letters display positive fury with the Austrian tyrants. Wherever he resided, he was an eyesore to the Austrian authorities; his letters were opened; the Italian translation of *Childe Harold* was prohibited in the Austrian provinces of Italy; and the police, as he well knew, were incited to assassinate him. Nevertheless, he calmly took his usual ride every day. On this, as on other occasions, his conduct and language were distinguished by a mixture of stoic heroism and boyish bravado. There is something attractively boyish in his writing to Murray:

I wonder if they can read my letters when they have opened them; if so, they may see, in my MOST LEGIBLE HAND, THAT I THINK THEM DAMNED SCOUNDRELS AND BARBARIANS, and THEIR EMPEROR A FOOL.

When proclamation was made that extremely severe penalties would be incurred by all in whose houses weapons were found, he stored the weapons of all the conspirators of the Romagna in his villa, which became a regular arsenal. The cupboards and drawers were crammed with the revolutionary proclamations and oath-formulas. He thought, and thought rightly, that the authorities would hardly dare to search the house of a member of the English House of Peers.

It was easier for them to drive him away than to imprison him; it was done simply by ordering the Counts Gamba to leave the country within twenty-four hours. It being one of the agreements of the separation that the young Countess was to be obliged, if she left her father's house, to enter a convent, the authorities felt sure that the step they were taking was a sure means of getting rid of Byron. Teresa's letter to her lover on hearing of this order ends thus:

Byron! I am in despair!—If I must leave you here without knowing when I shall see you again, if it is your will that I should suffer so cruelly, I am resolved to remain. They may put me in a convent; I shall die—but—but then you cannot aid me, and I cannot reproach you. I know not what they tell me, for my agitation overwhelms me; and why? Not because I fear my present danger, but solely, I call Heaven to witness, solely because I must leave you."[17]

---

[17] The long work, *Lord Byron Jugé par les Témoins de sa Vie*, which Countess Guiccioli published in 1868, though it does not really help us to understand either Byron's character or his art, bears touching evidence to the strength and depth of the Countess's love. The solution of the problem which the world calls Byron, is, for her, contained in one word: He was an *angel*—beautiful as an angel; good as an angel; an angel in everything. The 1100 pages of the book are divided into chapters bearing the titles of his different virtues; one is consecrated to his philanthropy, another to his modesty, &c., &c. The chapter upon his faults proves in the most satisfactory manner that he had none. The description given of his person corresponds to that of his character. We have separate disquisitions on the beauty of his voice, of his nose, of his lips. It is incomprehensible how such a shameful aspersion can have been spread abroad as that Lord Byron was lame or had a clubfoot. His limp was so slight that it was impossible to detect which foot caused it; and his lordship's shoemaker, who still owns the last on which his boots were made when he lived at Newstead, bears witness (his attestation being appended) to the slightness of the defect. It is equally incomprehensible how the foolish report can have found credence, that Lord Byron's hair had begun in his later years to recede from his forehead; certainly that part of his head was rather

The fortune into possession of which Byron came through his marriage, and which, strange to say, he had no scruples in keeping; another fortune, produced by the sale of Newstead; and the £20,000 which he had in course of time received from Murray in payment of his poems, had placed him in a position to exercise benevolence on a grand scale. When it was reported that he intended to leave Ravenna, the poor of the neighbourhood sent a petition to the Cardinal Legate that he might be allowed to remain. But it was this very devotion of the people to him that made him dangerous to the Government. He removed from Ravenna to Pisa. The Tuscan Government being quite as much afraid of Byron and the Gambas as was the Government of the Papal States, there was soon another expulsion, and the party proceeded to Genoa, Byron's last place of residence in Italy.

---

bare, but simply for the reason that he chose to have it shaved. Another unaccountable and foolish falsehood is the assertion that his legs grew very thin. Certainly they were thinner in the last years of his life than they had been when he was younger; but was that at all remarkable in a man who spent most of his leisure hours on horseback?—When we remember that this book was published forty-four years after Byron's death we cannot but acknowledge that the love which inspired it was strong and lasting.

XXII

CULMINATION OF NATURALISM

IN THE PERIOD BETWEEN 1818 AND 1823 Byron wrote *Don Juan*. Immediately after the first part of the manuscript reached England, he was inundated by communications from friends and critics who had been allowed to see it—expressions of consternation, entreaties to omit this or that, deprecations of the immorality of the poem. Immorality!—that was the cry Byron had to hear at each step of his life, and which pursued him after death; their immorality was made the pretext for burning his memoirs, and his immorality the pretext for refusing his statue a place in Westminster Abbey. Byron replies in a letter to Murray:

> If they had told me the poetry was bad, I would have acquiesced; but they say the contrary, and then talk to me about morality—the first time I ever heard the word from anybody who was not a rascal that used it for a purpose. I maintain that it is the most moral of poems; but if people won't discover the moral, that is their fault, not mine … I will have none of your damned cutting and slashing. If you please you may publish *anonymously*; it will perhaps be better; but I will battle my way against them all, like a porcupine.

This poem, which, with its savage dedication to Southey, had to be published, not only anonymously, but actually without any publisher's name on the title-page, and which, as Byron said, had more difficulty in making its way into an English drawing-room than a camel in passing through the eye of a needle, is the one poem of the nineteenth century which can be compared with Goethe's *Faust*; for it, and not the comparatively insignificant *Manfred*, is Byron's poem of universal humanity. Its defiant motto is the famous speech in *Twelfth Night*: "Dost thou think, because thou art virtuous, there shall be no more cakes and ale? Yes, by Saint Anne, and ginger shall be hot i' the mouth, too!"—a motto which promises nothing but offence and satiric pleasantry. Nevertheless it was with justifiable and prophetic pride that Byron said to Medwin:

> If you must have an epic, there's *Don Juan* for you; it is an epic as much in the spirit of our day as the *Iliad* was in that of Homer.

It was Byron who produced what Chateaubriand imagined he had produced in *Les Martyrs*, namely, the modern epic poem—which it was not possible to construct, as Chateaubriand had attempted to do, on a Christian-Romantic basis, or as Scott had thought it might be done, on the foundation of national history and manners. Byron succeeded because he took as his foundation nothing less than the most advanced civilisation of the century.

Juan is no Romantic hero; neither his mind nor his character raises him much above the average; but he is a favourite of fortune, an exceptionally handsome, proud, bold, lucky man, who is led more by his destiny than by intention or plan—the proper hero for a poem which is to embrace the whole of human life. It would never have done for him to have any special province; for, from the very beginning, there was no limit set to the scope and reach of the work.

The poem rises and falls like a ship borne upon sunlit and storm-tossed billows; it passes from one extreme to another. On the ardent love-scenes between Juan and Julia follows the shipwreck, with its horrors of starvation and its death agonies; on the shipwreck follows the splendid and melting harmony of youthful love—that highest, freest, sweetest happiness of life. Juan and Haidée are a study of the nude, as beautiful as an animate Amor and Psyche; above them the moonlit sky of Greece; in front of them the wine-coloured sea—the melodious lapping of its waves, the accompaniment of their words of love; around them the enchanting atmosphere of Greece; at their feet all the splendour of the East—scarlet and gold, crystal and marble. All this had followed upon peril and suffering; and now, upon the festival in Haidée's palace, follows such agony for Haidée that her heart breaks, and, as Juan's lot, a sabre gash on the forehead, crushing fetters, and sale as a slave. But it is to a seraglio he is sold, and presently we have the droll episode of his introduction, disguised as a girl, to the favourite sultana, and the mischievous night scene, with all its fire and fragrance, all its merry and voluptuous fun. Straight from this we are taken to the assault of Ismail—to human slaughter on the hugest scale, and to all the cruelty of a reckless war, carried on by a brutal soldiery—the whole described with more power and at greater length than any similar episode had been before in the poetry of any country. We next find Juan at the court of Catherine of Russia, among the "polished boors" of Eastern Europe, who are ruled by a gifted Messalina; and thence we follow him to England, the promised land of highway robbery, of morality, of the power of birth and wealth, of marriage, of virtue, and of hypocrisy.

This rough outline merely suffices to convey an idea of the capacious proportions of the poem. Not only does it contain, in extraordinary variety, representations of the strange contradictions in human life, but each of these contradictions is followed out to its extremest development. In each case the sounding-lead of the poet's imagination has been let down to the bottom, both in the psychological and in the external, tangible situation. Goethe's antique temperament inclined him, wherever it was possible, to moderation; even in *Faust*, where, in terrible earnest, he lifts the veil from human life, he lifts it with a careful hand. But the result of this moderation is often a deficiency in the highest potency of life. In Goethe's works the geniuses of life and death are seldom allowed unlimited space in which to spread their giant wings. Byron has never the desire to tranquillise his reader, never thinks of sparing him. He himself is not calm until he has said everything there is to say; he is a mortal enemy of the idealism which beautifies by selecting this, rejecting that; his art consists in pointing to reality and nature, and crying to the reader: Know these!

Take any one of his characters—take Julia, for instance. She is twenty-three; she is charming; almost without being aware of it, she is a little in love with Juan; she is contented with her husband of fifty, but also, almost unconsciously, has a faint wish that he could be divided into two of five-and-twenty. After a hard struggle to remain virtuous she gives way; but for a time there is nothing base or comical in the relations of the lovers. Then Byron shows her to us in a difficult position; the pair are surprised by the husband; and all at once we discover a new stratum of her nature—she lies, she deceives, she acts a part with astounding facility. She was not, then, good and amiable, as she at first appeared to be? We were mistaken? Not at all. Byron shows us yet another deeper-lying stratum of her soul, in the famous farewell letter she writes to Juan, an effusion of sincere womanly feeling, one of the gems of the poem. Mental agony does not incapacitate for devotion; love does not preclude deceit; nor deceit extreme delicacy and beauty of feeling at given moments. And the letter—what becomes of it? Juan reads it, sighing and weeping, on board ship; in the middle of its affecting comparison of the manner in which men love with that in which women love, he is interrupted—by sea-sickness. Poor letter, poor Julia, poor Juan, poor humanity!—for is not this human life? Once again, poor letter! After the shipwreck, when the crew of the boat have devoured their last ration and have long gazed hungrily at each other's famished figures, they agree to determine by lot which one of them shall be killed and eaten by the others. Search is made for paper, but not a scrap is to be found in the boat except Julia's poetical and loving letter; it is snatched from Juan and cut into squares, which are numbered. One of these numbered squares brings death to Pedrillo. Is there, then, really a sphere in the firmament of heaven where idealistic love and cannibal instincts are to be found side by side, nay, meet upon one square inch of paper? Byron answers that he knows one—the Earth.

From the shipwreck scene we are transported straight to Haidée. Compared with her, all the Greek maidens of Byron's earlier poems are immature attempts. Nowhere in the whole range of modern poetry had the love of a child of nature been so beautifully described. Goethe's best girl figures, Gretchen and Clärchen, charming as they are, are little *bourgeoises*; we feel that their creator was a Frankfort citizen, to whom nature revealed herself in his position as a member of the middle class, and culture displayed itself at a small German court. In Byron's most beautiful female characters there is nothing bourgeois—no middle-class manners and customs have modified their free naturalness. We feel, when we read of Juan and Haidée, that Byron is a descendant of Rousseau; but we also feel that his high and independent social position, in combination with the character of the fortunes that had befallen him, had given him a much more emancipated view of human nature than Rousseau ever attained to.

> And thus they wander'd forth, and hand in hand,
>   Over the shining pebbles and the shells,
> Glided along the smooth and harden'd sand,
>   And in the worn and wild receptacles
> Work'd by the storms, yet work'd as it were plann'd,
>   In hollow halls, with sparry roofs and cells,
> They turn'd to rest; and, each clasp'd by an arm,
> Yielded to the deep twilight's purple charm.
>
> They look'd up to the sky, whose floating glow
>   Spread like a rosy ocean, vast and bright;
> They gazed upon the glittering sea below,
>   Whence the broad moon rose circling into sight;
> They heard the waves' splash, and the wind so low,
>   And saw each other's dark eyes darting light
> Into each other—and, beholding this,
> Their lips drew near, and clung into a kiss;
>
> A long, long kiss, a kiss of youth, and love,
>   And beauty, all concentrating like rays
> Into one focus, kindled from above;
>   Such kisses as belong to early days,
> Where heart, and soul, and sense, in concert move,
>   And the blood's lava, and the pulse a blaze,
> Each kiss a heart-quake.   .   .   .
>
> .   .   .   .
>
> Haidée spoke not of scruples, ask'd no vows,
>   Nor offer'd any; she had never heard
> Of plight and promises to be a spouse,
>   Or perils by a loving maid incurr'd"

What reader (especially if he comes straight from the erotic hypocrisy of the literature of the French reactionary period) but feels carried away by this strong current of warm youthful passion, by the poet's ardent enthusiasm for natural beauty, and by his profound scorn for the prudishness of conventional morality! Is there, then, a world, a world of law in which 2 and 2 make 4, an animal world in which all the lowest and most disgusting

instincts may come to the surface at any moment, and yet in which such revelations of beauty in human life—revelations lasting for a moment, or a day, or a month, or a year, or an eternity of years—occur? Yes, answers Byron, there is such a world, and it is the world in which we all live. And now, away from these scenes to the slave market, to the seraglio, to the battlefield, to systematic murder and rape and the bayoneting of little children!

The poem is made up of such contrasts and contradictions. But it is not a sensuous, playfully satiric epic of the nature of Ariosto's; it is a passionate work, instinct with political purpose, full of wrath, scorn, threats, and appeals, with from time to time a loud, long blast on the revolutionary war trumpet.[18] Byron does not merely describe horrors; he interprets them. After quoting "the butcher" Suwarrow's rhymed despatch to Catherine announcing the capture of Ismail, he adds:

> He wrote this Polar melody, and set it.
>   Duly accompanied by shrieks and groans,
> Which few will sing, I trust, but none forget it—
>   For I will teach, if possible, the stones
> To rise against earth's tyrants. Never let it
>   Be said that we still truckle unto thrones;—
> But ye, our children's children I think how we
> Show'd *what things* were before the world was free!

If, considering both from this point of view, we compare *Don Juan* with *Faust*, the great poem of the beginning of the century, we feel that the strong, practical, historical spirit of *Don Juan* carries, as it were, more weight with it than the philosophical spirit which inspires *Faust*. And if we place it for a moment in imagination beside its Russian offspring, Pushkin's *Jevgeni Onjœgin*, and its Danish offspring, Paludan-Müller's *Adam Homo*, the fresh sea breeze of nature and fact in the English poem seems to us all the stronger in contrast with the polish and the political feebleness of the Russian, and the narrow morality of the clever Danish, poem. In *Don Juan* we have nature and fact; in *Faust*, nature and profound reflection. *Don Juan* gives us in full, broad detail the human life which *Faust* condenses into a personification; and the whole work is the production of an indignation which has written where it can be read by the

---

18   "I have prated
Just now enough; but by and by I'll prattle
Like Roland's horn in Roncesvalles' battle."

mighty of all ages its *"Mene, Mene, Tekel, Upharsin."*

Not until he wrote this work was Byron completely himself. The thorough experience he had now had of life had cured him of all youthful credulity. He knew now exactly what went to the composition of the average man, and what regulated that man's life. He has been called misanthrope because of his savage satire of such lives. He himself gives the proper answer to the impeachment (ix. 21):—

Why do they call me misanthrope? *Because They hate me, not I them?*

There is no doubt that he is occasionally cynical, but it is where nature herself is shameless.

Is he very far wrong when he says (v. 48, 49):

Some talk of an appeal unto some passion,
    Some to men's feeling, others to their reason;

.   .   .   .

                    no
Method's more sure at moments to take hold
Of the best feelings of mankind, which grow
    More tender, as we every day behold,
Than that all-softening, overpowering knell,
The tocsin of the soul—the dinner-bell.

Is he wrong when (ix. 73) he affirms love to be vain and selfish? Or does he let his satirical temper carry him too far when he says, in describing the happiness of family life (iii. 60):

Yet a fine family is a fine thing
    (Provided they don't come in after dinner);
'Tis beautiful to see a matron bring
    Her children up (if nursing them don't thin her).

Alas! as long as there is a wrong side to the most beautiful things, it is in vain to forbid the poet to show it to us, let the moralist groan as he will. These passages are among the most cynical in the poem. And it is to be remarked that the bitter, Rousseau-like attacks on civilisation (as the joys of which the poet enumerates "war, pestilence, the despot's desolation, the kingly scourge") are always accompanied by ardent declarations of love for nature (see especially viii. 61-68).

Byron exclaims (iii. 104):

Some kinder casuists are pleased to say,
    In nameless print—that I have no devotion;

.   .   .   .

    My altars are the mountain and the ocean,
Earth, air, stars, all that springs from the great Whole,
Who hath produced, and will receive the soul

But, unfortunately, natural religion of this kind was not in accordance with theological ritual. Like a refrain from *Childe Harold* recurs the glorification of liberty of thought (xi. 90):—

        I may stand alone,
But would not change my free thoughts for a throne.

There are savage attacks on the theory of the origin of sin advanced by theology, and satire of orthodoxy and its doctrine that sickness and misfortune make us good. Of sin we read (ix. 19):—

'But heaven,' as Cassio says, 'is above all—
    No more of this, then, let us pray!' We have
Souls to save, since Eve's slip and Adam's fall,
    Which tumbled all mankind into the grave,
Besides fish, beasts, and birds. 'The sparrow's fall
    Is special providence,' though how it gave
Offence, we know not; probably it perch'd
Upon the tree which Eve so fondly search'd.

We observe how much freer and bolder the tone has become since the days when *Cain* was written. On the subject of sick-bed orthodoxy Byron writes:—

    I don't know what the reason is—the air
Perhaps; but as I suffer from the shocks
Of illness, I grow much more orthodox.

The first attack at once proved the Divinity
    (But *that* I never doubted, nor the Devil);
The next, the Virgin's mystical virginity;
    The third, the usual origin of evil;
The fourth at once established the whole Trinity
    On so uncontrovertible a level,
That I devoutly wish'd the three were four
On purpose to believe so much the more.

Byron had now reached the stage in his literary career when he had difficulty in getting his works published. Murray was apprehensive, and drew back. Not even a bookseller was to be found who would sell the earlier cantos of *Don Juan* at the author's risk. Byron says, when comparing his own fate with Napoleon's (*Don Juan*, xi. 56):—

But Juan was my Moscow, and Faliero
    My Leipsic, and my Mont Saint Jean seems Cain:
'La Belle Alliance' of dunces down at zero,
    Now that the Lion's fall'n, may rise again.

We have already noted what Southey dared to say in the preface to his servile poem, *The Vision of Judgment*. Adopting the rôle of informer, he called upon the Government to prevent the sale of Byron's works—for that his attack was upon Byron he plainly avowed in his rejoinder to Byron's answer, triumphantly boasting:

Of the work which I *have* done, it becomes me not here to speak, save only as relates to the Satanic School, and its Coryphæus, the author of *Don Juan*. I have held up that school to public detestation, as enemies to the religion, the institutions, and the domestic morals of the country. I have given them a designation *to which their founder and leader answers*. I have sent a stone from my sling which has smitten their Goliath in the forehead. I have fastened his name upon the gibbet, for reproach and ignominy, as long as it shall endure.—Take it down who can!

Thus wrote the retained and salaried scribbler, who, as Byron says, had lied himself into the post of Poet-laureate. Byron replied in his admirable satire, HIS *Vision of Judgment*. In it, as in Southey's vision, George the Third arrives at the gates of heaven and requests to be admitted. But Saint Peter is not at all willing to open for him. The locks and keys are rusty; there has been so little doing; since 1789 every one has been going to hell. Cherubs arrive to insist on the old man's being admitted—for all the angels are Tories. But Satan makes his appearance as accuser, and he and Saint Michael dispute possession of the dead man. Both produce witnesses, and amongst others Southey is called. Southey begins to read his own works aloud, and goes on so long that all, angels and devils, take flight, and in the general confusion the old King slips into heaven. Saint Peter upraises his keys and knocks the poet down with them:—

Who fell, like Phaëthon, but more at ease,
Into his lake, for there he did not drown;
.   .   .   .
He first sank to the bottom—like his works,
    But soon rose to the surface—like himself;
For all corrupted things are buoy'd like corks.

The little masterpiece is imposed on exactly the same lines as the poem of Southey's which it parodies.[19] The difficulty was to get it printed. Murray would not accept it, nor would any other London publisher.

It was while he was in this dilemma that Byron was guilty of the literary imprudence which injured him more than any other in the estimation of the English reading public. A talented, but not much respected man, the Radical author, Leigh Hunt, whom Byron as a young man, to show his politics, had (in company with Moore) visited when he was in prison for libelling the Prince Regent, and who was now on terms of intimacy with Shelley, conceived the idea of starting a Radical periodical in collaboration with Shelley and Byron. Shelley, out of modesty, held back himself, but no sooner had he intimated to Hunt that there was a possibility of his obtaining Byron's assistance, than Hunt gave up all his occupations and chances of earning a living in England, and landed, penniless and helpless, with wife and family, in Italy, where Byron generously gave them shelter under his roof. But it soon became evident that no real community was possible between two men of such different natures and different calibre; Byron could not stand Hunt's indiscreet familiarity; Hunt was offended by Byron's haughtiness. But the worst misfortune was, that Byron sank incredibly in the estimation of his countrymen by this alliance with such an inferior man.

In vain did Thomas Moore, when refusing to contribute to the proposed journal, write:

"I deprecate such a plan with all my might … You are, single-handed, a match for the world—which is saying a good deal, the world being, like Briareus, a very many-handed gentleman—but, to be so, *you must stand alone*. Recollect that the scurvy buildings about St. Peter's almost seem to overtop itself."

---

[19] For other attacks on Southey, see *Don Juan*, i 205; iii. 80, 93; ix. 35; x. 13.

Byron had promised to help Hunt, and would not be induced to take back his word. He little thought that, after his death, Leigh Hunt's first action would be to write three volumes with the purpose of sullying his fame.[20] He gave him *The Vision of Judgment* and *Heaven and Earth*, the grand poem on the destruction of the world by the Flood, to which we Danes trace a likeness in Paludan-Müller's *Ahasuerus*. But the periodical, which it was originally proposed to call *The Carbonari*, but which, from political reasons, came out under the feeble name of *The Liberal*, was received with such complete disapprobation that it was given up after only four numbers had appeared. The arena of literature was thus almost closed for Byron, and the only field that really remained open to him was that of action, of war, in the literal sense of the word, for his ideas.

But before embarking on this new venture he gave his revolutionary feelings vent in *Don Juan* and *The Age of Bronze*. Shelley considered that Byron was qualified by his ambition and his powers to be "the redeemer of his degraded country." But he was mistaken; Byron was little suited to take part in the obstinate, slow struggle of the English Opposition for liberty. Besides, it was not the political predicament of England alone that aroused his sympathies and occupied his thoughts; in his revolt against all oppression and hatred of all hypocrisy he made himself the spokesman of the whole suffering world. His blood boiled when he thought of the slaves in America, of the ill-treatment of the Irish lower classes, of the martyrdom of the Italian patriots.

Of the French Revolution Byron had always approved. He admired Napoleon in the first stages of his career; but when the hero of the age passed:

---

[20] Thomas Moore aptly compares Hunt to the dog which was allowed by the lion to live in his cage, but which, after the lion's death, had nothing but evil to say of him:—
"Though he roar'd pretty well—this the puppy allows—
    It was all, he says, borrow'd—all second-hand roar;
And he vastly prefers his own little bow-wows
    To the loftiest war-note the lion could pour.
.   .   .   .
Nay, fed as he was (and this makes it a dark case)
    With sops every day from the lion's own pan,
He lifts up his leg at the noble beast's carcase,
    And—does all a dog, so diminutive, can."

The Rubicon of man's awaken'd rights,
    To herd with vulgar kings and parasites,

and finally, at Fontainebleau, preferred abdication to suicide, he overwhelmed his quondam ideal leader with the fiercest satire. There is much resemblance between Byron's attitude towards Napoleon and Heine's. Both pour ridicule on the so-called wars of liberation waged against him by their respective countries. The great difference is, that the Englishman's inflexible pride and his devotion to liberty made it impossible for him to lose himself in the almost feminine admiration and enthusiasm by which the German was possessed. Napoleon's military fame made no impression on the man who has beautifully said (*Don Juan*, viii. 3) that:

The drying up a single tear has more
    Of honest fame, than shedding seas of gore;

and who admired no warriors but those who, like Leonidas and Washington, fought for freedom.

Byron had long flourished his lash above the Prince Regent's head, and many a telling stroke had fallen upon that royal personage's fat body:— "Though Ireland starve, great George weighs twenty stone." "Charles to his people, Henry to his wife," &c. Now he took the country itself to task. His lash falls upon everything false and objectionable, from the legend of the Virgin Queen, "our own half-chaste Elizabeth," as he calls her in *Don Juan* (ix. 81), down to the latest requirements of public opinion (*Don Juan*, vii. 22):

Then there were Frenchmen, gallant, young, and gay;
    But I'm too great a patriot to record
Their Gallic names upon a glorious day;
    I'd rather tell ten lies than say a word
Of truth;—such truths are treason.

He is daring enough to attribute great part of the honour of Waterloo to the Prussians; to call (in imitation of Béranger) Wellington "Villainton," and to tell him that he has obtained great pensions and much praise for doing nothing but "repairing Legitimacy's crutch." And with a feeling and fervour far surpassing that displayed by Moore in his satirical letters, he tells England of the hatred of herself which she has aroused in other nations by her Tory politics. "I've no great cause," he writes (*Don Juan*, x. 66):

I've no great cause to love that spot of earth,
   Which holds what *might have been* the noblest
        nation;
But though I owe it little but my birth,
   I feel a mix'd regret and veneration
For its decaying fame and former worth.
   .   .   .   .

Alas! could she but fully, truly know
   How her great name is now throughout abhorred;
How eager all the earth is for the blow
   Which shall lay bare her bosom to the sword;
How all the nations deem her their worst foe,
   That worse than *worst of foes*, the once adored
False friend, who held out freedom to mankind,
And now would chain them, to the very mind;—

Would she be proud, or boast herself the free,
   Who is but first of slaves? The nations are
In prison—but the gaoler, what is he?
   No less a victim to the bolt and bar.
Is the poor privilege to turn the key
   Upon the captive, freedom? He's as far
From the enjoyment of the earth and air
Who watches o'er the chain, as they who wear.

Byron had now reached the altitude at which all ordinary conventions lost their hold upon him. He pursued the "Ministry of Mediocrities," as he called it, with his satire even after the death of its members. He would not let Castlereagh rest quietly in his grave, because, as he says in one of the prefaces to *Don Juan*, the system of oppression and hypocrisy with which that statesman's name is synonymous, endured long after his death. The watchword of the day, sovereignty "by the grace of God," was obnoxious to him, as was also the perpetual recurrence of the phrases: Britannia's rule of the waves, the glorious British constitution, the noble Emperors, and the pious Russian people. On the coins of gold appear once more, he writes after the fall of Napoleon, faces with the old "sterling, stupid stamp." The universal idolisation of the most uncivilised nation of Europe disgusted him. One could not go anywhere at that time without hearing the sentimental Cossack's song of farewell to his sweetheart, the first words of which, "Schöne Minka," are not yet forgotten.

Thus it was Byron who, towards the middle of the twenties, inaugurated the Radical campaign against political Romanticism and that Holy Alliance which was nothing but a systématisation of the political hypocrisy of Europe. Byron called it:

An earthly trinity! which wears the shape
Of heaven's, as man is mimicked by the ape.
A pious unity! in purpose one—
To melt three fools to a Napoleon.

He jeered at "the coxcomb Czar, the autocrat of waltzes and of war." He ridiculed the "twenty fools" at Laybach, who imagined that their hypocritical proceedings could determine the destiny of the human race. He cried:

O Wilberforce! thou man of black renown,
   Whose merit none enough can sing or say,
Thou hast struck one immense Colossus down,
   Thou moral Washington of Africa!
But there's another little thing, I own,
   Which you should perpetrate some summer's day,
And set the other half of earth to rights;
You have freed the *blacks*—now pray shut up
     the whites.

Shut up the bald-coot bully Alexander!
   Ship off the Holy Three to Senegal;
Teach them that 'sauce for goose is sauce for gander,'
   And ask them how *they* like to be in thrall?

What language! What tones breaking the death-like silence of oppressed Europe! The political air rang with the shrill notes; for no word uttered by Lord Byron fell unheard to the ground. The legions of the fugitives, the banished, the oppressed, the conspirators, of every nation, kept their eyes fixed upon the one man who, amidst the universal debasement of intelligences and characters to a low standard, stood upright, beautiful as an Apollo, brave as an Achilles, prouder than all the kings of Europe together. Free, in his quality of English peer, from molestation everywhere, he made himself the mouthpiece of the dumb revolutionary indignation which was seething in the breasts of the best friends and lovers of liberty in Europe.

He himself had defined poetry as passion;[21] and inspired passion was what his own became. Listen to some of the thunders that pealed over Europe:

---

[21] Poetry, which is but passion." *Don Juan*, iv. 106.

You hardly will believe such things were true
  As now occur, I thought that I would pen you 'em;
.   .   .   .
And when you hear historians talk of thrones
  And those that sate upon them, let it be
As we now gaze upon the mammoth's bones,
  And wonder what old world such things could see.
                    (*Don Juan*, viii. 136, 137).

Think if then George the Fourth should be dug up!
  How the new worldlings of the then new East
Will wonder where such animals could sup!
                    (*Don Juan*, ix. 39).

But never mind;—'God save the king!' and kings!
  For if *he* don't, I doubt if *men* will longer—
I think I hear a little bird, who sings
  The people by and by will be the stronger:
The veriest jade will wince whose harness wrings
  So much into the raw as quite to wrong her
Beyond the rules of posting—and the mob
At last fall sick of imitating Job.

At first it grumbles, then it swears, and then,
  Like David, flings smooth pebbles 'gainst a giant;
At last it takes to weapons such as men
  Snatch when despair makes human hearts less
      pliant.
Then comes 'the tug of war;'—'twill come again,
  I rather doubt; and I would fain say 'fie on't,'
If I had not perceived that revolution
Alone can save the earth from hell's pollution.
                    (*Don Juan*, viii. 50, 51).

And I will war, at least in words (and—should
  My chance so happen—deeds), with all who war
With Thought;—and of Thought's foes by far most rude,
  Tyrants and sycophants have been and are.
I know not who may conquer: if I could
  Have such a prescience, it should be no bar
To this my plain, sworn, downright detestation
Of every despotism in every nation.
                    (*Don Juan*, x. 24).

XXXIII

BYRON'S DEATH

H E HAD PROPHESIED REVOLUTION; he had sorrowfully witnessed the failure of the plans laid by the Carbonari; but now at last the expected revolution had begun.

On Andes' and on Athos' peaks unfurl'd,
The self-same standard streams o'er either world.

He had been expelled from the ranks of literature in England. He had been driven from town to town in Italy. It had long been a saying with him that a man ought to do more for his fellow-men than write poetry, and over and over again had he talked of art with the contempt of a Hotspur. Now everything conspired to urge him to action. Consideration for the Countess Guiccioli alone restrained him. He had thoughts of taking part in the Creoles' struggle for liberty; he made careful inquiries into the condition of matters in South America. His *Ode on Venice* ends with the words:

> Better be
> Where the extinguish'd Spartans still are free,
> In their proud charnel of Thermopylæ,
> Than stagnate in our marsh—or o'er the deep
> Fly, and one current to the ocean add,
> One spirit to the souls our fathers had,
> One freeman more, America, to thee!

The attraction to the country which had first inspired him to song proved the strongest. He tore himself away from the Countess Guiccioli, who was anxious to accompany him, but whom he dared not expose to the dangers and hardships of a campaign. The Committee of the English friends of Greece had elected him their representative, and supplied him amply with funds. On the day of his departure from Leghorn he received his first and last greeting from Goethe, in the shape of the old master's famous sonnet to him.

For five months he continued to reside on the island of Cephalonia, occupied in carefully investigating into the real state of matters in Greece, and besieged by the different Greek leaders, who were at enmity with each other, and each of whom was eager to enlist Byron on his side. The distribution of money, ammunition, and other materials of war necessitated an immense amount of correspondence, to which Byron attended with dogged industry. He at last made his choice among the Greek leaders, determining to join Prince Mavrocordato at Missolonghi. During his stay in Cephalonia proposals had been made to him which must have been most flattering to his ambition. The Greeks had a strong bias towards monarchical government, and Trelawny, who was in a position to know, was convinced that, if Byron had been alive at the time of the Congress of Salona, the crown of Greece would have been offered to him.

When Byron landed at Missolonghi he was received like a prince. The fortress fired a salute, bands played, the whole population crowded to the shore to welcome him. At the house prepared for his reception, Mavrocordato awaited him at the head of a staff of officers, both Greek and foreign. Five thousand armed men were quartered in the town. Byron took five hundred Suliotes (natives of Albania), who had been left leaderless by the death of Marco Bozzari, into his own pay. He selected for himself, as if death were what he desired, the most dangerous of the commands, that of the troops which were to proceed to Lepanto, hoping to compensate by energy and courage for his want of military experience; his staff were to be responsible for the strategical direction of the force. He had occasion, while holding this command, to be astonished by the powerful impression which personal accomplishments and personal intrepidity make upon half-savage natures; nothing produced such respect for him in the minds of his Suliotes, who themselves were bad marksmen, as his unerring aim and his indifference to danger. But he had undeniably become a nobler man. Though not free from attacks of his old melancholy, he saw the path of glory clear before him. Evidence of his feeling at this time is borne by the beautiful poem, one of the finest he ever wrote, which he composed on his thirty-sixth birthday. If we compare it with the despairing lines which bear the date of his thirty-third birthday, the difference is clearly perceptible. Along with premonition of his approaching death we have manly resolve:—

'Tis time this heart should be unmoved,
 Since others it hath ceased to move:
Yet, though I cannot be beloved,
  Still let me love!

My days are in the yellow leaf;
 The flowers and fruits of love are gone;
The worm, the canker, and the grief
  Are mine alone!

. . . .

But 'tis not *thus*—and 'tis not *here*—
 Such thoughts should shake my soul, nor now,
Where glory decks the hero's bier,
  Or binds his brow.

The sword, the banner, and the field,
 Glory and Greece, around me see!
The Spartan, borne upon his shield,
  Was not more free.

. . . .

Seek out—less often sought than found—
 A soldier's grave, for thee the best;
Then look around, and choose thy ground,
  And take thy rest.

Byron's very first endeavour was, as might have been expected of him, to modify, as far as possible, the barbarity of the method in which the war was being carried on. He released several Turkish officers, and sent them to Yussuf Pacha with a dignified and beautiful letter, in which he begs him in return to treat such Greeks as may henceforth fall into his hands with humanity, since the horrors of war are sufficiently great without being aggravated by wanton cruelties on either side. Then he turned all his attention to the task he had set himself, and displayed a clear-sighted practicality which stood out in marked contrast to the poetical visionariness of those with whom he was associated.

The other Englishmen of the Committee, in their unworldly idealism, hoped to civilise Greece by means of a free press, newspaper articles, &c., &c.; but in Byron, the Carbonaro had made way for the practical politician. He built everywhere, energetically and firmly, upon the actually existing conditions—first and foremost upon the hatred of Turkey which existed in the breast of every Greek. He considered it much safer to reckon upon this than upon their devotion to freedom and republicanism. Stanhope wished to open schools. Byron demanded and distributed cannon. Stanhope endeavoured, through the agency of missionaries, to introduce Protestant Christianity. Byron, who saw that this foolishness would alienate the whole Greek priesthood, would have nothing introduced but weapons and money. And he left off making attacks upon the different European Governments. He had witnessed the collapse of Carbonarism when brought into contact with organised authority; hence his desire was to obtain for Greece recognition by the Great Powers.

Unfortunately his health was not equal to the carrying out of his great plans. At Missolonghi he rode out as usual every day, and, to impress the inhabitants, was always attended by a bodyguard of fifty Suliotes on foot. These men were such splendid runners that, though they carried their carbines, they were able to keep up with the horses galloping at full speed. On one of these rides Byron was drenched by a heavy shower. Count Gamba tried to persuade him to return home at once, but he refused, saying:

I should make a pretty soldier, indeed, if I were to care for such a trifle."

The following day he was seized with violent convulsions—three men were hardly able to hold him—and the pain was so excessive that he said: "I do not care for death, but these agonies I cannot bear." While he was lying in an almost fainting condition after this attack, a band of rebellious Suliotes made their way into his room, brandishing their sabres, and demanding reparation for some supposed slight. Byron raised himself up in bed, and with a powerful exercise of will, ever calmer the more they raged and screamed, mastered them with his look and manner, and dismissed them.

He had written to Moore some months previously:

If anything in the way of fever, fatigue, famine, or otherwise, should cut short the middle age of a brother warbler, I pray you to remember me in 'your smiles and wine.' I have hopes that the cause will triumph; but whether it does or no, still 'honour must be minded as strictly as milk diet.' I trust to observe both.

On the 12th of April he had again to take to bed, and from this date the fever never abated.

The 18th was Easter Day, a holiday which the Greeks were accustomed to celebrate by firing off muskets and salvos of artillery; but out of consideration for their benefactor, the townspeople kept perfectly quiet.

The 19th was the last day of Byron's life. During part of it he was delirious; he imagined himself to be commanding troops, and shouted: "Forwards—forwards—courage!"

When he came to himself again, he began to give his last orders to his servant, Fletcher. "Go to my sister," he said; "tell her—go to Lady Byron—you will see her, and say—."

Here his voice became indistinct, and only names could be made out—"Augusta—Ada—Hobhouse."

He then said: "Now, I have told you all."

"My lord," replied Fletcher, "I have not understood a word your lordship has been saying."

"Not understood me?" exclaimed Lord Byron, with a look of the utmost distress. "What a pity! Then it is too late; all is over."

He still continued to utter a few disconnected words: "Poor Greece!—poor town!—my poor servants!"

Then his thoughts must have turned to Countess Guiccioli, for he murmured: "Io lascio qualche cosa di caro nel mondo."

Towards evening he said: "Now I shall go to sleep," and, turning round, fell into that slumber from which he never awoke.

The announcement of Byron's death fell like a thunderbolt upon Greece. It affected the nation in the manner of a terrible natural catastrophe, the consequences of which were incalculable. On the day he died the following proclamation was issued:—

PROVISIONAL GOVERNMENT OF WESTERN GREECE.

The present day of festivity and rejoicing has become one of sorrow and of mourning. The Lord Noel Byron departed this life at six o'clock in the afternoon, after an illness of ten days ... I hereby decree:—

1st, To-morrow morning at daylight, thirty-seven minute guns will be fired from the grand battery, being the number which corresponds with the age of the illustrious deceased.

2nd, All the public offices, even the tribunals, are to remain closed for three successive days.

3d, All the shops, except those in which provisions or medicines are sold, will also be shut; and it is strictly enjoined that every species of public amusement, and other demonstrations of festivity at Easter, shall be suspended.

4th, A general mourning will be observed for twenty-one days.

5th, Prayers and a funeral service are to be offered up in all the churches.

A. MAVROCORDATO.

Given at Missolonghi this 19th day of April 1824.

No other evidence is required of the impression which the news of Byron's death made upon all who were intimately connected with him. At Missolonghi people ran through the streets crying: "He is dead! The great man is gone!" The corpse was conveyed to England. The clergy refused it a place in the Poet's Corner in Westminster Abbey. But, dependent neither on the blame of England nor the praise of Greece, his renown established itself throughout the earth.

In the intellectual life of Russia and Poland, of Spain and Italy, of France and Germany, the seeds which he had strewn broadcast with such a lavish hand fructified—from the dragon's teeth sprang armed men. The Slavonic nations, who were groaning under tyrannical rule, who were by nature inclined to be melancholy, and in whom their history had developed rebellious instincts, seized on his poetry with avidity; and Pushkin's *Onjœgin*, Lermontoff's *A Hero of Our Own Days*, Malczewski's *Marja*, Mickiewicz's *Conrad* and *Wallenrod*, Slowacki's *Lambro* and *Beniowski* witness to the powerful impression made upon their authors. The Romance races, whose fair sinners his verses had celebrated, and who were now in the act of revolt, eagerly translated and studied his works. The Spanish and Italian exile-poets took up his war-cry; in Spain the "Myrtle" Society was formed; in Italy his influence was most plainly manifest in the writings of Giovanni Berchet, but hardly less so in those of Leopardi and Giusti. His death made an extraordinary impression in France. A week or two after it happened, Chateaubriand went over to the Opposition, and his first action after his fall was to become a member of the Greek Committee. Hugo's *Les Orientales* was not a flight straight to the East, like the Oriental poetry of Germany; his way lay through Greece, and he had much to say of the heroes of the war of liberation. Delavigne devoted a beautiful poem to Byron; Lamartine added a last canto to *Childe Harold*; Mérimée allowed himself to be influenced by Byron's occasional spirit of savagery; Alfred de Musset attempted to take up the mantle which had fallen from the shoulders of the great poet; and even Lamennais began to employ a style in which many of the words and expressions recalled the language of Byron's sallies. Germany was still politically too far behind the other nations to have exiles and emigrants among its poets; but its philologists had, with quiet rejoicing, beheld in the rising of Greece the resurrection of ancient Hellas; poets like Wilhelm Müller and Alfred Meissner wrote beautiful verse in honour of Byron; and there were other writers who were still more deeply moved by Byron's poetry—men of Jewish extraction, whose feelings were those of the exiled and excommunicated—chief among them Börne and Heine. Heine's best poetry (notably *Deutschland, ein Wintermärchen*) is a continuation of Byron's work. French Romanticism and German Liberalism are both direct descendants of Byron's Naturalism.

XXIV

CONCLUSION

NATURALISM AS AN INTELLECTUAL tendency in England, makes its appearance in Wordsworth in the form of love of all the external phenomena of nature, a habit of storing up natural impressions, and piety towards animals, children, country people, and the "poor in spirit." With him as its representative, it strays for a moment into a blind alley, that of uninspired imitation of nature. In Coleridge, and even more in Southey, it approaches the German Romanticism of the day, follows it into the world of legend and superstition, but avoids its worst excesses by treating Romantic themes in a Naturalistic manner and keeping an open eye on land and sea and all the elements of reality. In Scott, Naturalism occupies itself with the character and history of a whole nation, and in vivid colours paints man as the son of a race and a period; in Keats, it takes possession of the whole world of the senses, and reposes for a moment on the neutral ground between tranquil contemplation of nature and the proclamation of a gospel of nature and of natural rights. In Moore it becomes erotic, and espouses Liberalism in politics; the sight of the sufferings of his native island drives this poet into the ranks of the lovers of liberty, intellectual and political. In Campbell, it becomes eulogy of England as Queen of the Sea and expression of English liberal views. In Landor, it takes the shape of pagan Humanism, of too repellent and proud a character to win the suffrage of Europe. It is transformed in Shelley into a soulful love of nature and a poetic Radicalism, which have at their command poetic gifts of the very highest order; but the incorporeal universality of Shelley's Naturalism, in combination with the circumstance that he is much too far ahead of his age, and with his early death, causes his song to die away unheard, Europe never learning what a poet she possesses and loses.

Then, like Achilles arising in his wrath after he has burned the body of Patroclus, Byron, after Shelley's death, arises and lifts up his mighty voice. European poetry was flowing on like a sluggish, smooth river; those who walked along its banks found little for the eye to rest on. All at once, as a continuation of the stream, appeared this poetry, under which the ground so often gave way that it precipitated itself in cataracts from one level to another—and the eyes of all inevitably turn to that part of a river where its stream becomes a waterfall. In Byron's poetry the river boiled and foamed, and the roar of its waters made music that mounted up to heaven. In its seething fury it formed whirlpools, tore itself and whatever came in its way, and in the end undermined the very rocks. But, "in the midst of the infernal surge," sat such an Iris as the poet himself has described in *Childe Harold*—a glorious rainbow, the emblem of freedom and peace—invisible to many, but clearly seen by all who, with the sun above them in the sky, place themselves in the right position.

It presaged better days for Europe.

THE END

Biography & Criticism

Oxford Lectures on Poetry
Hegel's Theory of Tragedy, Wordsworth, Shelley. Keats, Shakespeare
A. C. Bradley

Shakespearean Tragedy
Hamlet, Othello, King Lear, Macbeth
A. C. Bradley

Friedrich Nietzsche
George Brandes

William Shakespeare - A Critical Study
George Brandes

John Keats
Sidney Colvin

Prophets of Dissent:
Essays on Maeterlinck, Strindberg, Nietzsche, Tolstoy
Otto Heller

Henrik Ibsen: Plays and Problems
Otto Heller

Lectures on Dramatic Art and Literature
August Wilhelm Schlegel

The Quintessence of Ibsenism
G. Bernard Shaw

Percy Bysshe Shelley
John Addington Symonds

& more

Check the website for more books
(new titles added weekly)

mannwilliam.org

Printed in Great Britain
by Amazon